GOOD STORIES AND HOW TO TELL THEM

Good Stories
and How to Tell Them

A Collection of Appropriate Stories for Speakers
with Instructions About the Best Way to Tell Them

by
V. SPENCER GOODREDS

Publishers

T. S. DENISON & COMPANY

Minneapolis

Printed in the U. S. A.

By THE BRINGS PRESS

International Copyright Secured

Library of Congress Catalog Card Number: 58-11750

The Library of Congress catalog entry for this book appears at the end of the text on page 250

Dedication

*This book is the result
of encouragement given me
by my audiences.*

Contents

SECTION ONE

SECTION TWO

Contents *(Continued)*

Foreword

As a teacher of speech and an active speaker for more than twenty-five years, I think it is safe to say I have examined or completely read (and in some instances made slight use of) many of the volumes of stories, jokes and anecdotes published each year.

For the most part, these publications are collections designed to serve as repositories to be dipped into by speakers of many types who have need for a story which may seem appropriate for use as suggested by the topical arrangement of the stories. Basically, they are practical reference books from which speakers can select stories to use in speeches and in everyday social, business and professional affairs. Beyond this, such volumes as a whole have little usual book value or interest. Aside from their utility value the stories may have individual appeal, but they do not constitute related interest or over-all appeal in the sense of sustained book interest from beginning to end. Perhaps, such books need no more continuity of appeal than does a *Bartlett's Familiar Quotations*.

In presenting the material of this book it is expected that it will be employed as a source for speakers and also by those people who cultivate stories for social use. In addition, since it is designed to be read, it is hoped it will be enjoyed by those who enjoy reading amusing, serious and sometimes inspirational stories and anecdotes for pleasure, and that the material has related and sustained interest from beginning to end.

Most of the stories are humorous; some are serious. Many

are gay; none is risque. Many of the anecdotes are unusual incidents from the lives of well-known personalities such as Robert Frost, the poet, Joe DiMaggio, Katherine Cornell, John Mason Brown, Paul Dwight Moody and Bishop Charles E. Brent among others, whom the author, through the years, has known intimately.

Some essential speech techniques and commentary or rules, which have a definite relationship to good storytelling, constitute an important part of the book's material. In addition, special mention is made preceding each chapter regarding the interest and value of the chapter content, and interspersed among the stories is comment as to their nature and special use.

It is realized in order to have sustained book interest it is essential to have coherence of chapters. Such continuity is not easy to attain when chapters have topical significance as is evident in this volume. Based on respect for good composition, however, an attempt has been made to maintain coherence within the chapter to heighten its appeal by having the stories definitely related and by use of transitional comments between them. If interest is held in a chapter, it is hoped the subject matter may create curiosity in reading subsequent ones.

The first section of the book is devoted to speech techniques of special value to the speaker and storyteller. This section of the book can be used independently by those who make speeches, or who act as speech chairmen, who wish to improve their knowledge and use of principles which apply to better speaking. It has been especially written for any use made of the second part of the book composed of several chapters of stories.

Regarding the subject matter of the stories included in the volume, there are five main categories of social, human or work-a-day interest, with stories drawn from the fields of education, religion and government and two, concerned with our leisure time activities, drawn from sports and the entertainment field. In addition there are two groups of stories with instructional comment, one for speech chairmen and another especially for speakers. To round out the book there is a section devoted to *Miscellaneous Stories,* including a group of general items and another dealing with the humor of *The British Isles.*

I am reminded of the spirit of Somerset Maugham's remarks used in his novel, *Then And Now,* when he says, in substance, that no one could write a book of this kind completely out of his head. Therefore I have used or adapted some of the stories from other sources I had available.

Wherever there is a debt to outside sources, for any material or stories, full credit has been recognized. Special acknowledgements are to be made to John Mason Brown, author of *Accustomed As I Am,* a Norton publication, for material adapted from its pages and to George Dixon for use of material from his syndicated column, *Washington Scene.*

Every attempt has been made to present a book which has unique value in its field. It is hoped that in some degree, the attempt has been successful.

—V. Spencer Goodreds

CHAPTER ONE

The Humorous Story

Give me a sense of humor, Lord,
Give me the grace to see a joke
To get some happiness from life,
And pass it on to other folk.

—From a tablet in England's
Chester Cathedral

The great American pastime, aside from attending sports events and the "movies," seems to be, as expressed in the vernacular, "to make the joke." At the banquet table, in the pulpit, over the radio, in social gatherings, at club meetings, and in the classroom the popular vogue is to tell the humorous story. It is indulged in by the best minds and by the rank and file of people, and for the benefit of each other; it is the great leveler of society.

It is not too much to say, that the good will and fellowship engendered through the humor of the story in America is a true manifestation of the democratic spirit; it is the basic element of democracy. In keeping with this thought, Erich Brandeis, a prominent columnist, recently wrote, "One magnificent asset of our people is not mentioned in the history books. Yet it is one of our greatest natural assets—one in which . . . we excel all other people . . . and which keeps the United States great. That asset is a sense of humor." To which he adds, "As long as we can laugh, we are invincible. The atomic bomb may be a great weapon for war, but a sense of humor is a greater one for peace." And before we conclude these observations, I am prompted to add that I recently read an article written by Dave Garroway, the television performer, entitled: "If the Russians Would Only Learn to Laugh." I think some of his comments are worth restating. He observes: "The Russian people are not without a sense of humor . . . Tolstoi and Turgenev wrote great comic passages in their novels and stories, and Chekhov some appealingly humorous lines in such masterpieces of comedy as 'The Cherry Orchard.'

"However, the cherry orchards got chopped down when the Revolution came—and so did the comedians. *I never*

*heard of a dictator with a sense of humor, and the Communist
dictators, past and present, are no exception.*

"Already one quarter of the world is behind the Humor-
less curtain.

"Restore a sense of humor to the Communists and you'll
restore enlightened civilization to 800,000,000 people.

"One of the world's greatest tragedies was that Karl Marx
never met the Marx Brothers.

"When the current Russian premier can begin a speech
with the Russian version of 'Who was that lady I saw you
with last night?' instead of the exhortation, 'Comrades,' all
of mankind can smile.

"What worries me so much about the Communists' lack of
humor is that it may spread to our country . . . One of our
finest symptoms of freedom is our ability to crack jokes at
our government's expense. Republicans make fun of Democrats, Democrats kid Republicans. When we're afraid to be
funny about our political opponents, there won't be any politics left, just dictators.

"The only invasion of Russia that I would like to see is an
invasion by comedians like Milton Berle, Groucho Marx, Bob
Hope, and Jack Benny."

Bob Hope's visit there is, by this time, a realization.

Democracy, then, is basically a happy spirit, which cannot be embraced by sad minds or depressed individuals. In
this connection, it is significant to pause and note that Americans, for this reason, will never adopt a political philosophy
that, in its ideology, represses the happy spirit in man. And
for this reason, if for no other, the humorous story will be,
and should be, told whenever people are gathered together.

OTHER TYPES OF STORIES

Because humor does not always, or only, lurk in the story, conversely the story to be effective does not always have to contain humor; that is humor that calls forth enjoyment in laughter. Many stories have their appeal because of human interest elements, a peculiar twist in the wording, or through satire; others because of new and novel ways of presenting situations, or in pure concreteness, and because they are graphic. Such stories are not always or essentially funny, but more often they depend upon the appreciation of a quieter and inward response.

I recently heard a Washington clergyman hold a commencement audience literally spellbound. He told many stories which were thoroughly enjoyed, none of which contained humor; they were, however, rich in human interest, and greatly heightened the appeal of his address.

A good storyteller does not, or should not, depend on the humorous story alone. Good books, good plays, good talks and good conversation are all designed for pleasurable appeal to all the emotions, and likewise a story should be employed as a medium to satisfy and appeal to all the emotions. It should not, therefore, be restricted to one type.

Most of the stories included in this volume were selected to have an humorous appeal. Others which may have virtue and interest because they highlight, or throw in bold relief, fine characteristics and worthy traits of human nature, have also found a place in the book. It is hoped these stories will serve as a solid nucleus for those interested in building up a collection of stories for effective speech making. It is further and more especially hoped that this volume, and its comments relative to the humorous story, will encourage its readers to begin a systematic method for collecting stories, which is a "must" for every successful storyteller.

HOW TO COLLECT STORIES

There are certain worth-while practices and methods which can be cultivated, to advantage, if a person is to develop a good supply of stories.

WRITE THE STORY DOWN

Invariably among people the remark is heard, "I never can remember a story." This is not surprising when no effort is made to try and remember one. Too often, when hearing a story, a person trusts it to his memory, and he finds when he wants to tell it, it has fled completely. Psychology has established the fact that we forget one half of all we hear within ten minutes, and an amazing per cent of the remaining half within a week. We think we can remember; but our memory is treacherous. To remember things, we must hog-tie them; to remember stories, we must write them down. It may not always be possible to write a story down at the time we hear it told, but it should be written down at the first and earliest opportunity. It is not necessary, in order to remember a story, to write it down verbatim. It is important to get the main ideas and, above all, to get the punch line absolutely straight. Then at a later time it can be rewritten and the details of the narrative filled in with your own words. Don't worry if it varies slightly from the original version. If it reads well and flows into the climax or punch line, which must be correct, the chances are a good story will have been added to your collection.

It is almost axiomatic that the best stories are still of the "hand to mouth" variety, or those transmitted orally. Good stories may often appear singly in magazines or in newspapers, but it seems a collection or anthology of consistently good stories is yet to be printed. After stories are written down in good legible form, it is well to arrange them topically in a file, which once started will develop an interest to continue building up the collection.

CULTIVATE BROAD SOURCES

The potential storyteller, however, must constantly cultivate possible sources where stories may appear that he can use. He should scan the various sections of the newspaper, not necessarily confining his search to sections devoted to humor or those most likely to include the humorous anecdote, but read all the columnists who may discuss life, the theater, religion, politics, society or education for possible hidden stories, or gems of humor which may be adapted into stories. A further consideration of adaptation of material will be made later in the chapter.

SUGGESTED SOURCES

Trade magazines, organs or publications of large business and manufacturing organizations serve as splendid sources because they make a specialty of including a department of anecdotes and humorous stories. Religious denominational magazines and church publications are especially lucrative sources, and the writer has found the monthly publications of insurance companies to be rich in such material. The magazines of the service organizations, Kiwanis, Lions, and Rotary all pride themselves on being able to amuse their readers with good laughs. The speaker who is active in his search for stories knows the value of these sources and many others. It is suggested that the stories or material found to be of interest should be clipped and pasted on three by five cards and then inserted in a topically arranged file.

RESEARCH

In particular reference to the collection and use of stories I am reminded of a story which seems especially appropriate. It came from the keen mind of the late Nicholas Murray Butler, president of Columbia University.

Dr. Butler and one of his eminent professors, Brander Matthews, a reasonably keen wit himself, were having a conversation and Professor Matthews was giving his ideas about plagiarism from an article of his own on that subject.

"In the case of the first man to use an anecdote," he said, "there is originality; in the case of the second there is plagiarism; with the third, it is lack of originality; and with the fourth it is drawing from a common stock."

"Yes," broke in President Butler, "and in the case of the fifth, it is research."

And here Dr. Butler, not discounting the humor of the situation, could have been making a point in all seriousness for the potential storyteller. He must cultivate every source possible if he is to develop a collection of stories, which, literally amounts to research.

CHAPTER TWO

The Use of Stories
and How to Tell Them

. . . I dote upon a jest
Within the limits of becoming mirth.
—Hood

Most speakers, who are not experienced, assume, in order to be effective, that they must be funny; and to be funny that they must tell many humorous stories. To them, this is their main purpose and complete responsibility as a speaker.

As a teacher of speech, and with some years of experience as a speaker and master of ceremonies, I have many calls from individuals who are to speak or serve as master of ceremonies requesting stories to use. They have, it is true, in many instances, been concerned about what to do in order to be an effective speaker or chairman. It is principally because of such requests that these suggestions have been written.

It is not to be assumed that the speaker or master of ceremonies should refrain completely from using stories. The important question he must ask himself in regard to their use is: what is the motive for using stories? Is it to satisfy a personal desire to be funny? Therein lies the danger. To be funny "per se" as an end in itself cannot but serve to detract from the purpose of the program as a whole. To make the story serve an independent purpose beyond its definite relation to a speech or a program is fundamentally bad technique. Shakespeare wisely admonishes all those who seek to be funny for their own sake, when he says ". . . let those who play your clowns speak no more than is set down for them, for it shows . . . a most pitiable ambition in the fool who uses it."

Finally, it may be said the humorous story has its place if certain definite criteria are observed.

If a story is not irrelevant to a speech and a program, generally, and may appropriately enhance their purpose it has value.

If, however, it affects the mood or even tenor of a speech

and program by not being in harmony with them, it should not be used, no matter how well it may be rated as a story.

If it unduly prolongs the length of a speech or a speaking program and digresses from the main purpose of either, it should, likewise, not be used. Even though it may be a proved laugh-getter, it may not be appropriate.

If it has any stigma of the personal, and may embarrass another speaker or a member of the audience, it should not be used.

The over-all, complete and final test for its use is: is it appropriate?

Illustrative of the choice of stories is my young son's favorite story, which no doubt he has heard the famous Joe Laurie, Jr. recount. It concerns itself with the chairman, on the occasion of a dinner, who arose and began the introduction of the first speaker by saying:

"Ladies and gentlemen: I shall not take your time tonight by boring you with the telling of old stories or 'chestnuts,' but I shall be very happy to introduce speakers who will."

This little statement, by humorous indirection, embodies a rather important consideration about the selection of stories to tell, whether they may be too old or whether they are good or bad. And here it seems advisable to say a word regarding the use of stories in respect to both of these considerations.

As to the retelling of presumably good or acceptable stories, audiences are keen and do not like to hear the same story too often. Be sure your stories are new and have not lost their appeal; otherwise, replenish your stock. Remember, people are constantly being talked to or bumped into by others who make a business of telling only stories they have heard, and they have no compunctions about doing so. They never engage in research or any other activity which will mark them as original in the use of stories. I recently heard a lady say, "I've heard four clergymen within the last month all tell the same story." So many people who think they are speakers stand up and tell the story they heard at the last Rotary Club meeting or the like, being totally unmindful that others, perhaps, have heard the story before and since. It is absolutely stupid and insulting.

Most audiences laugh when they hear a story, but don't be too sure it is because of the story; it may be just politeness. As Shakespeare says in *Macbeth*; "There is no art to find the mind's construction in the face."

NEW STORIES AND OLD STORIES

While current publications and the popular newsstand magazines very often reveal material or stories, there is the resulting possibility that the humorous items they contain will find a corresponding popular use among people, generally, who tell stories. The user must be careful or he will find the new story he uses has, because of its wide distribution, other users, and many people who are familiar with it. The latest Bennett Cerf story and others reprinted in the *Reader's Digest*, or elsewhere, may be hearty laugh-getters when first told or first read, but they stand an excellent chance when retold of being perfect "duds." Therefore, it may not be advisable to use stories for which there is a wave of early interest; they have more appeal if they are allowed to lie fallow for a while. I have heard stories told three or four years after they have appeared which, with some modification, have been well received. I would not, generally, advise

using old stories in preference to new ones, but in this respect
I like, in slight paraphrase, the thought of Alexander Pope,
the English essayist, who says,

"Be not among the first by whom the new are tried,
Nor yet the last to lay the old aside."

Use stories promptly after you have heard them, before
everyone has a chance to become familiar with them; or wait
until you are reasonably sure people have had a chance to
forget them. Cultivating both methods will insure you of a
fund of usable stories. It is not essential that the storyteller's
repertoire be made up entirely of stories which are new or
up to date.

RETELLING POOR STORIES

Mark Twain's observation about cigars may *apply* to
stories, when he says, "A good cigar should be lighted once,
a bad one never." A good story can stand being retold, but
not to the same audience. Perhaps the safest guide to follow
about telling a bad story is, never tell it. Certainly never
retell it because it cannot always be determined in advance
if a story is bad. A story may be poor for several reasons. It
may be weak in appeal, or simply no good; it may not be appropriate, or it has not been well told.

There is usually little doubt about the effectiveness or
appeal of a story. The narrator definitely knows by the audience response whether his story is well received or not. If it
is not, he can readily sense it. The speaker can readily sense
if the story is not appropriate, or if it is not well told. He
should profit by experience.

KNOW THE STORY — KNOW THE PUNCH LINE

It is important that when a story is used it should be well
told. Nothing is worse than to have listeners subjected to a

story that is poorly told, because the one who recounts it is not sufficiently familiar with it and garbles the details. So, our advice to those who tell stories is, *be sure you know the whole story. Know the beginning so you get started well. Know how it develops to the climax and the punch line, and know how to end it. When you reach the end, stop.* Nothing has a worse effect on the telling of a story than to be indefinite about the ending or to add an anti-climax. Nothing, that is, unless the punch line is not clearly told. *Know the punch line!*

BE SURE YOU HAVE TERMINAL FACILITIES

Too many speakers often spoil an otherwise acceptable speech or story by not being able to bring it to a close. They lack a sense or need of terminal facility.

Lew Sarett, the poet and unusual speech teacher at Northwestern University, offers a sage bit of counsel to speakers in his book "Basic Principles of Speech," about ending a speech. It applies equally to those who tell stories. Interestingly the idea was suggested to him by Paul Whiteman, who in proposing techniques for conducting an orchestra said, ". . . when you quit, quit all over." Sarett admonishes the speaker thus: ". . . every speech when it quits should quit all over."

Aristotle, the Greek scholar, proposed that a speech, among other things, to be a complete organism must have a head, body and feet, or a beginning, middle and end.

This important principle applies to the telling of a story. Know the beginning; know how to develop it; and, most important, know the ending. When you get there, end it. Don't try to embellish it with added remarks. When you quit, quit all over.

OTHER POINTERS FOR THE STORYTELLER

To tell a story well, there are other admonitions which it may be well to point out here as particular knowledge for the speaker. They are equally important for the toastmaster.

1. Don't stretch the story out or make it too long. Even if the point of the story is well told, it will not justify stretching it out by unnecessary verbiage, as the listeners' interest will be lost by the time you get to the point of the story.

2. Don't give the point of the story before you actually begin to tell it. Many a novice completely kills the interest in a good anecdote by announcing the story in a phrase which reveals pretty much its whole idea, such as: "Now I would like to tell you the story about . . . ," or, "This reminds me of the story of the Bishop who explained to the French chorus girl the meaning of the golden wedding anniversary, and she thought it meant a man can live with a woman fifty years before he marries her."

    No, a good storyteller launches into his story without thunder, as a good mystery story writer builds up suspense and saves the solution for the end.

3. Don't tell a story at the wrong place or on the wrong occasion. A story which may be told to certain individuals, or a few friends in a confidential way, may fall flat to the point of being resented in a formal audience. Many stories are considered by most audiences to be risque to the point of the indecent, but too often the people who tell them don't seem to know that. Some individuals are not safe before an audience, when it comes to telling stories. They just don't

know the social psychology of audiences. The guiding principle is, "Is the story appropriate for the occasion?"

One of the best known contemporary storytellers has summed it up this way: "The man who can toss off a funny story in the right spot is a wit; the oaf who is telling them indiscriminately all the time is a nitwit."

RETELLING STORIES IS NOT ENOUGH. PROPER INTERPRETATION AND THE ABILITY TO ADAPT IS REQUIRED

A good storyteller must do more than collect and remember stories in their original form for retelling. Otherwise, the true technique of storytelling will not be cultivated or developed, and his repertory may be limited.

He must develop the real art of the storyteller which is the art of interpretation, about which more will be said. And secondly, and closely allied to interpretation, he must develop the technique of adaptation—the ability to adapt or develop humorous items, sayings and situations into possible story form. He must have a ready sense for recognizing usable or adaptable material for the improved story. Many stories have been created from a humorous situation or commentary, which is proved by the history of humor. The basic situations from which humorous stories are derived or are developed, are limited; but the applications of them are numerous. They are all variations of six or seven basic themes. In the field of playwriting for example, it is generally believed that there are from three to seven situations upon which the plots of plays are built and from these few situations the whole wealth of dramatic material has developed. The humorous story is in essence a small play, and as such, depends upon new or different treatment of a basic idea for its narrative.

The creation of a story or the adaptation of a humorous situation into a particular story form, and the expert telling of it, represent the two aspects of successful comedy in the field of entertainment today. The "Bob Hopes" of radio and television may be reasonably expert in telling stories and recounting situations in humorous monologues, but the creation of the humorous situation into suitable form is the business of the comedian's writer, who is the figurative head and brain of the collaborating team, while the comedian is the mouthpiece.

The storyteller or master-of-ceremonies in the public speaking situation, or the after-dinner speaker, who is not in the professional field of entertainment, has no such an arrangement with a co-worker.

It is true he cultivates sources for stories and story material which aid him and, therefore, he is not a creator in the strict sense of the comedian's writer. He must, however, use his own ingenuity in determining what stories to use and how to adapt certain other material for use. It is likewise true the comedian may have something to say about the choice of his material and he may collaborate in the preparation of it, but he never works alone either in securing or preparing it. The storyteller, who is the non-professional, must develop both techniques, that of the creator or adapter, and also the interpreter. Therefore, unless he becomes adept in both of these phases of the storyteller's art, he will never be successful before audiences, who expect and demand this ability.

THE STORYTELLER'S STOCK-IN-TRADE

To be a good storyteller, then, is not a lazy or a dull man's job. It presupposes a lively, alert interest in cultivating myriad sources for possible material, a discerning intelligence and a creative imagination in selecting and using the material, and finally, the knowledge or techniques for interpretation together with the expressive media of voice and personality, both essential and indispensable aids. The opportunity for constant practice is, of course, an absolute requirement if one is to become an expert interpreter.

THE TECHNIQUE OF INTERPRETATION

Good interpretation is concerned with good speech and diction. As Shakespeare says, "Speak the speech, I pray you. . . . trippingly on the tongue, for if you mouth it, . . . I would as lief the towncrier spoke my lines," is sound advice for anyone who speaks lines before an audience. The purpose of all speaking or reading is to communicate ideas to listeners. There is no other purpose. The principal aim of the storyteller is to communicate every single word of the narrative he tells, if the listeners are going to understand the story. This presupposes well-articulated speech or clear diction, coupled with adequate voice volume if one is to be heard.

These elements are basic in good interpretation. Of course it includes also all the elements of good speech in addition to those already indicated. It is assumed the story teller has reached reasonable perfection in the techniques of speech, particularly pronunciation, tempo, rhythm and voice inflection. This does not mean that the art of the storyteller or the interpreter is the art or technique of the public speaker, even though they have much in common.

GOOD EXPOSITION — MAKING ALL DETAILS CLEAR

Proper interpretation requires a definite care in emphasizing or clearly pointing out the important elements of the narrative, such as names of characters and other details necessary to the understanding of the story or its plot. Sometimes the punch line or climax of a story is not understood or appreciated because previous details, upon which the point of the story depends, are not clearly revealed. This is what is known as a lack of clear exposition.

How often have we come away from a movie disturbed or half satisfied with the picture because we failed to understand the entire plot? And why? Because some details upon which its understanding was dependent were not included, were not clearly or audibly revealed, or were spoken during laughter of the audience.

To accomplish these things places a three-way responsibility upon the storyteller:

1. Include all the necessary details or expository device necessary to the understanding of the plot.
2. See to it that these details of exposition are clearly revealed by clear and audible speech; that is, don't garble them by inadequate or poor expression.
3. Don't try to explain them if the audience is laughing at other comments you have just made. That is, don't talk through the laugh lines.

St. John Irvine, the British dramatic critic, emphasizes the importance of item one in his small book entitled "How To Write a Play," which could be read to advantage by every storyteller.

He is talking about the dramatist who attempts to adapt the basic narrative form, the novel, into a play (or a movie)

for the theater audience. He decries the practice of not including sufficient explanation necessary to the understanding of the story. He says, ". . . adapters nearly always assume that the audience has read the novel and is intimately familiar with its details. So they leave great gaps in the story, as if they were saying to themselves, "Well, I needn't put that bit in. The audience is sure to know about it.' " The storyteller likewise assumes that the audience will understand certain things without explanation or details, and that is where he is wrong.

To highlight the importance of item two, we can draw again from the theater; as the actor's art, for the most part, is the art of storytelling.

As a young man I was a member of a theatre stock company whose director, working under William Brady, the noted producer, was always concerned about the actors reading their lines carefully and clearly. Occasionally when an actor failed to make clear some important dialogue concerning character or story detail, the director would yell out, "Plot! Plot!", which was a reminder to the actor to make it clear as this was information the audience must get if the story was to be understood.

Comments about item three are considered in the following remarks on the use of the pause.

THE IMPORTANT PAUSE

Clear exposition, an essential element of effective interpretation, also requires the judicious use of the pause, as the narrator unfolds the story. The listener only hears the story once and the use of the pause before and after an important point aids its emphasis. The pause before a point primes the listener for what is to come, and the pause after it gives sufficient opportunity for complete comprehension.

Another important need for the pause is for laughs. A cardinal principle in the actor's technique, when he is playing comedy, is not to talk between or during the laugh lines. Our modern radio or television comedians are reasonably adept in pausing for laughs. Sometimes they are not as subtle as they might be and the purpose of the pause is then too obvious. The technique requires that the use of the pause be almost unnoticeable. As one commentator on humor expresses it: "Pausing for laughs without seeming to do so is one of the most important things that you have to do when trying to get them. Unless you give your audience time to laugh, its members will 'dry up' on you because each person will keep quiet in trying to hear what you have to say next." The pause cannot be dragged out or held too long. Pause sufficiently to give the audience time to laugh, then pick up the narrative before the laughter completely dies. This is what is known as sensing the psychological moment, which must be regarded or otherwise the pace and rhythm of the delivery will be affected and may cause a resulting break in the listener's interest.

The storyteller may not have to pause as often as the comedian or monologist for laughs, because the average humorous story draws its laughs mainly from the punch line, but sometimes oftener. If the story is reasonably long it may not be advisable to depend solely upon a single laugh at the climax. As one writer has said, "Arrange a few minor laughs along the way while you work toward the big punch line at the end." But the use of the pause is essential so as not to crowd ideas too rapidly upon the listener.

CARRYING THE AUDIENCE ALONG AND AIDING THE LAUGHS

The comment is often heard "he always laughs at his own jokes." To do so may seem unwise if overdone, or if the basis for laughter isn't always clear to the audience. It is not effective when you start telling a story to indicate by your manner that it is a sure fire laugh-getter, and you know without a doubt that it is going to be funny. Let the audience determine if it is really funny. But it is still necessary to say something about aiding the laughs. Professional comedians know that a story cannot carry itself and they are adept at the business of carrying the audience along. They reveal a full appreciation of the points of the story as they relate it. They register by facial expression, vocal quality and good spirit a funny reaction at the proper time which makes certain the audience knows when to laugh. This is tantamout to saying that here is the point of the story or here is the climax. This also shows a proper sense of audience psychology.

This plan of carrying the audience along and aiding its reaction cannot be overdone or it may be harmful. As Shakespeare wisely admonishes, ". . . o'erstep not the modesty of nature; for anything so overdone is from the purpose of playing . . . for, this overdone, or come tardy off, though it make the unskillful laugh, cannot but make the judicious grieve. . . ."

EXPRESSION SHOULD NOT BE OVERDONE

While interpretation in story telling may have the quality of dramatic interpretation, which suggests vivid expressiveness, it must not and should not be theatrical or exaggerated in dramatic effect. It must be natural with the proper quality of restraint, which is true of all good public speaking and dramatic performance or acting.

The storyteller's art, therefore, carries with it no need for personal exhibitionism on the part of the storyteller himself. He is merely the interpreter, the medium of expression, and he is not to assume that he is more important than what he tells. If he projects himself to the point where attention is upon him rather than upon what he is saying or trying to get across, his purpose will be affected. His manner should never carry with it any suggestion of the performer attitude of, "how am I doing?"

On the other hand a speaker or storyteller can at no time be casual or too informal in his physical manner or delivery. As one authority expresses it, "informality can at times invite failure." A casual manner can reflect itself in the audience, which may fail to sustain interest and therefore its response is affected.

The real interpreter, while guarding against any tendency toward the over dramatic or personal show, must by his physical manner, vocal tones and quality and general demeanor suggest positiveness and poise if he is to be convincing. It suggests belief in himself, but not an unhealthy egotism. It is rather the confidence of the true performer in himself and in his material.

THE BEST ELEMENTS OF CONVERSATION

It is said that true and vital speech has for its norm the conversational mode, which means the manner of the speaker in relation to his audience, is characterized by the best elements of conversation; its ease, intimacy and sincerity. This manner, and only this manner, will insure the storyteller of the desired interest of his audience; assuming, of course, he has, in the first place, complete control of his material.

The best example for the speaking manner, which is neither too formal nor yet too informal, seems to be found in the technique of the leading announcers of the radio and television networks. The commentary regarding the commercials, heretofore, was formal and spirited, and the announcer, as far as his listeners were concerned engaged in a "pumping in" process. He usually stood up. Today the shift seems to be to an intimate friendly relationship with his audience. The announcer's whole manner seems to express personal and sincere interest, a me-to-you process. He often is seated; he is more convincing. He is establishing what is known as rapport, defined as "an intimate or harmonious relation, in accord or affinity." Roland Hayes, the eminent Negro singer, has well expressed the spirit of rapport. He says, "when I sing ten thousand people sing back." If the speaker, and particularly the storyteller, fails to establish rapport, a two-way process between speaker and audience, he fails to establish audience response.

GREAT ART CONCEALS ART

Finally, the true interpreter by the natural and instinctive use of technique is disarming in his influence upon his listeners. The control and instinctive use of technique makes him so natural that the audience fails to realize that this is artistry. When someone told the famous actress, Ethel Barrymore, that she was just being natural in her acting she remarked that being natural was the result of years of training in technique. The great theater director, Arthur Hopkins, said that a well-directed play never reveals the hand of the director, and so it is in all fields of accomplishment. In the field of golf the well-known Bobby Jones amazed people with the ease he executed his golf shots; the answer, of course, was hidden technique.

To be successful as a storyteller, one must know all the techniques enumerated and yet be so in control of them that they are not revealed as a conscious process. He employs them instinctively and with ease and facility, so they in no way interfere with his main purpose, which is interpreting the story for audience response. His whole conscious process is directed toward this end.

CHAPTER THREE

Speech Techniques
Which Apply

All attempts at exciting the feelings must prove ineffectual unless they be enlivened by the voice of the speaker, by his look, and by the action of almost his whole body.

—Quintilian

It must be observed that the effective use of the physical and pantomimic expressions or transitions in speaking involves physical and facial means which augment the spoken word. And more, they tend to animate and vivify it. The other transitions, the vocal and literary, by special means which will be indicated, likewise extend and amplify the purpose of basic speech.

Nothing has been said about the means to use more effectively the physical and pantomimic expressions. It may be advisable to set down their most important uses even though speakers attempt their use without employing proper techniques. The comment to follow will also attempt to include specific techniques to be employed.

The body as a unit, or by separate use of its parts, may communicate or express the speaker's thoughts, either with the spoken word or apart from it. Used apart from the vocal expression it has strength in serving as a transition between thoughts; to effect change, to accentuate or emphasize an idea; to punctuate thought elements and generally to serve as an aid in interpretation. And as previously mentioned, in such wise, it fills the pauses. It fills the pauses only if the body is used to augment the spoken word and is thereby a medium of communication. For it is basic technique in the art of public speaking, and also acting, that there should be no movement without a purpose and bodily actions should not be used indiscriminately. Physical and other transitions serve or should serve as supporting and added means of manifestation to heighten the value of the spoken word. This has to be true if the body is to serve as an effective agent of communication.

UNNECESSARY MOVEMENT AFFECTS GOOD SPEECH

Aside from activity essential for the novice in aiding the release of nervous tension and emotion, speakers should not engage in unnecessary movement. Such movement tends to detract from and interfere with the ideas and purposes of a speaker's message. To repeat, speaking is a total bodily process and every part of the body or organism which contributes to the expression of an idea should be consciously directed and coordinated to that end, until it becomes natural for the body and its parts to operate as an expressive unit—*toute d'une piece*—or the body as one piece.

PROPER PHYSICAL TRANSITIONS

A speaker may very effectively emphasize a transition in thought by the body. He can move forward to project the idea with definite steps, so the movement suits the word. This is body transition.

He may move forward and bend the trunk or torso toward the audience in definite emphasis, and as a natural extension of the trunk activity include the head as the physical climax of that activity.

It may be, and most naturally so, that in a desire to use the head in physical transition to emphasize and accentuate an idea, it is necessary to bend the trunk; but the head is the important physical agent of communication or transition. Coordination and use of the bodily parts in such cases are inevitable.

The practice in the use of one part of the body entails the use of others, and ease and facility develop in using the body as an effective means of communication.

There are numerous ways in which the body may be used to effect transitions in speech and interpretation and it is essential that the storyteller or speaker study the uses if he is to be a good interpreter.

FACIAL EXPRESSION ESSENTIAL TO ALL INTELLIGENT SPEECH

In speaking it is basic that the face should be the index of an animated body, an alert mind and the accompanying emotion in the manifestation of all communicative or expressive activity. This indicates complete coordination of the body and harmony of feeling in regard to the expression. This must be so if the communication of ideas is to be convincing to the audience. None of us is sufficiently adept in acting to be able to feel one way about something and to act another. Of course, the technique of effective pantomime is an art in itself, of which all good actors make a special and intense study. It is likewise important that speakers and interpreters, especially storytellers, do likewise. The use of the facial expression to manifest the idea and the attitude heightens their value. Without it full and proper interpretation is not accomplished.

THE HEAD — A DOMINANT MEDIUM OF EXPRESSION

The head is the seat of mental intention; it can readily manifest the perception of an idea. In the communicative process it is natural that the head becomes an active agent of expression. Good speakers employ the head to complement the spoken word by using it to give emphasis or to accentuate an idea. It can be used effectively to punctuate thought elements and to give the suggestion of finality. Correlated with the head activity, of course, is active facial expression of an idea. But as previously indicated this is essential in all bodily activity concerned with expression, for psychologically the face reflects both body (physical and emotional) and mental behavior. Knowledge and practice improve the quality of this behavior essential to vital interpretation.

For those who would become expert in the interpretation of the spoken word it is well to watch artists and speakers who use the head and face as active media of interpretation. In addition there should be full realization that for most expressed concepts or ideas there should be an attempt to manifest accompanying physical and facial transitions, and need to practice them whenever possible.

GESTURES

A natural part of physical expression to aid and convey meaning is the use of gestures. No gesture, however, is effective which does not grow out of the general physical activity, which in turn stems from the mental attitude and the bodily feeling or emotion. Actually then, the gesture must coordinate itself with the mental and emotional and expression becomes psycho-neuro-muscular activity or the body operating as one piece. A gesture cannot be tacked on or be a thing apart from the activity. As the observation is made of the British actress, Florence Kemble, she was the most *toute d'une piéce* (the body as a unit) actress the world had known. When she put on her glove, she did it with her whole body. This is the secret of all successful gesture. Any gesture is of the entire body.

Shakespeare partly conveys the idea of coordination of physical activity in acting when he says, "suit the action to the word, the word to the action . . . ." He, of course, understood the full implication of body relation.

Students and other speakers often express a desire to employ a gesture in a certain part of a speech. The determining factor as to its use should always be, what is the expression for which it is to be used and what feeling does it or can it generate? If it does not suit the word or correlate itself with the attitude or feeling, it cannot be used. The phrase suiting the action to the word has a fuller connotation than we are concerned with here. The important thing to remember is that a gesture should not be used for gesture's sake alone, but must relate itself to the expression in thought and feeling, and this means complete harmony, especially in respect to timing and execution. One almost invariable general rule to remember is that the action or gesture should precede the word. Words are usually the last part of the communication code. We first react physically to an idea, then complete the transmission of the thought by putting it into words.

Speak the following with gestures to experience the truth of this:

There goes the culprit now.

Leave here at once!

THE NATURAL AND STANDARDIZED GESTURES

The control of gestures in relation to speech becomes a reasonably attainable art when it is realized that when properly used, gestures are limited, and are practically standardized without being stereotyped.

Basically all gestures are included in or are derived from the following categories:

The hands or hand supine. Hands relaxed and naturally extended in front of the body with palms up in varying positions to suggest the idea or spirit of appeal, heightened by proper facial expression. This form of gesture has the quality and suggestion of friendliness and spiritual value. It asks

for favorable reception of an idea. It is an open hand gesture.
Example: We offer you this plan in all sincerity.

The hands or hand prone. The hands are extended forward in a reasonably relaxed manner, depending upon the nature of the transition, with palms down, to suggest the idea of suppression, to hold down or to keep quiet or control something. It is an open hand gesture.
Example: Take it very easy; this thing may blow up in your face.

The hands or hand index. Usually made with the hand by curling up the last three fingers and thumb and using the index finger to point out toward the audience. The hand is held at an angle. The gesture is mostly used to point out or to single out.
Example: There, right there, you are absolutely wrong.

The hands or hand vertical. Hands or hand extended forward in a vertical position to indicate a division or separation, and to differentiate one point or item from another. It is an open hand gesture with the hand straight out in a vertical position and the palm facing in.
Example: The elite here, the non-elite here. (Showing a division or separation)

The hands or hand averse. Hands extended out and palms turned up and out suggesting aversion to, an act of turning away or holding back or to stop, in the manner of a traffic policeman.
Example: The idea is completely repulsive.

The fist gesture. A commonly employed gesture, made with the fist tightly clenched. It is employed to carry the idea of strong emphasis, determination and possibly combat and denunciation. It is always made with emphasis.

Example: This thing is a must.

These are the main and natural gestures employed by speakers. They all involve the same or similar arm movements. The arm movements include approach or preparatory stroke to the desired height or position of the gesture, at which point the climax of the gesture is executed. Then there is the return of the arms to the normal or natural position.

THOSE IMPORTANT SPEECH TRANSITIONS

Reference has been made to the speaker's need for the effective use of physical and pantomimic transitions, those physical and facial aspects which better convey or augment the spoken word. Actually the speaker who will attain complete success in the art of communication with an audience must know and employ the four forms of transition. Without them the spoken word is reduced to its bare and primary meaning. Effective speech, which will motivate an audience, challenge its imagination and have the necessary emotional and aesthetic appeal, requires that the spoken word take on added or connotative meanings. And this is what the use of transitions can accomplish or, more specifically, are designed to accomplish.

In addition to the physical and pantomimic transitions set down above, and as essential in the physical aspects of speech, it is important to include here the other two forms of transition at the speaker's command, the literary or composition and the vocal. And since they relate to each other, we will find they help to explain each other.

In fact, while each of the transitions requires specialized techniques for its complete mastery, its effectiveness does not lie simply in using it individually or separately, but in combination with the others.

While the inexperienced speaker may instinctively employ transitions in his speech delivery, it might be well to list them specifically and include a word of explanation about how they serve to improve a speaker's communication, so he may become more adept in their use.

It may help, even now, if we make clear the exact meaning of "transition" as it is employed.

A transition may be expressed as a device or means of passage from one place to another, a change; the period, place, or passage in which a change is effected.

A device for filling in; a stage of development. A modulation, especially a transient modulation. This, of course, would particularly apply to the voice and could be a change in key.

In the communicative arts a transition serves, or may be thought of, as a supporting, added or amplified means of manifestation.

THE LITERARY TRANSITION

The literary transition is employed in the speech or composition itself. It is a verbal means of connecting or indicating a change in ideas. The use of it makes it easier for the audience to follow the ideas successively by aiding their coherence.

The effective use of the literary or verbal transition presupposes some knowledge of the basic principles of composition. And this is as it should be; for a cardinal principle of public speaking is: a good speaker is, first, a good user of the English language.

Verbal links or literary transitions can be single words such as "however" and "moreover;" they can be phrases such as "in light of this observation," "examining the other side of the question," or full sentences such as: "Now let us consider another important aspect of the subject." Sentence transitions are most effectively used at the end or beginning of paragraphs to set off the definite development of ideas. These three types may be expressed in various ways, depending on how they are intended to serve.

Whole paragraphs may be employed as transitions for distinct rhetorical value. And rhetorical value means speech value. While the literary transition in speech is primarily composition, it is basically or should be thought of as expressed discourse, as should the whole composition. Written speeches are designed for delivery. In other words, a speech is not a speech until it is presented or heard by an audience. A speaker may profit by his study and knowledge of English, but the ultimate test of his literary style is, how well does it impress and communicate thoughts to listeners?

And that is why the four forms of transition should be considered collectively. They are inextricably related to the purposes of effective speech. The literary transition in the speech composition is negligible until it is spoken, which brings us to the next one in their logical importance of use.

THE VOCAL TRANSITION

Actually the vocal transition is the literary transition given meaning by the means of voice techniques. In a prepared or manuscript speech the transition is there; to heighten its purpose requires proper use of the voice. It may not always be true or necessary, however, that the good speaker in order to employ vocal transitions must have them indicated in written form. The degree to which he employs them otherwise depends on how closely he follows a manuscript, the effectiveness of his communication without them, and his

.ability to use them. It is true that the most effective transitions are inherent in the composition or manuscript.

To effect passage from one idea to another without losing the relationship requires control of any one or a combination of speech techniques. It can be a change in the pitch level or vocal register to indicate to the listener a change in thought; a commonly employed vocal device. It can be a marked change in tempo or rate of an expression used also to signalize thought change. Any such expressions may be accompanied by increased vocal force or energy and most always by change in vocal quality.

The vocal transition alerts the listener to thought change by the use of sound variety. It breaks up sameness in speech patterns or the possibility of monotony to the ear and therefore heightens listening. It has practical value in that it makes for facility in hearing; expressions are clearly and readily understood.

VARIETY ALONE NOT ENOUGH

Variety in the use of the main characteristics of speech, rate, volume, pitch and quality is not sufficient in itself to constitute effective communication, or transitions. This can become a mere concern for the mechanics of speech; and a disregard for the ideas being expressed, and the attitude toward these ideas and the purpose of speaking.

EXPRESSIVE QUALITIES OF VOICE NECESSARY

Since the function of speech is to convey meanings to the mind of the auditor, the most effective voice is one that is completely responsive to the attitudes, moods and purposes of the speaker.

Changes of pitch, loudness, tempo and quality, necessary in meaningful and animated speech, require a high degree of co-ordinated and flexible psycho-neuro-muscular activity. This is primarily dependent upon control of muscular tension and relaxation, but the physiology concerned is too complex to attempt an explanation here.

In all voice and speech training the close relationship between speech and the intellectual and emotional processes must be recognized. As the individual thinks and feels, so he speaks. If his speech lacks variety and expressiveness, this reflects a lack of discriminating thought and a degree of emotional repression. The individual is not likely to read or speak with meaningful skill and variety, indicating relationships between and among ideas he is expressing, if he is not aware of them. Words or ideas which have no significance for the speaker will not be spoken with significance.

It must be recognized then that the answer to vital and adequate expression involves both an intellectual grasp of what is being spoken and a complete sensitivity of its deeper significance.

Any individual who would make his personality felt through the medium of voice must realize that speech, besides being a medium for influencing human behavior through the communication of purely intellectual concepts, is most effective when it also reflects feelings, attitudes, or convictions.

The speaker who has a flexible, responsive voice for use in the speech generally should have no trouble effecting clear-cut motivating vocal transitions, which are the ever-recurring guide posts to the main purposes of a speech.

AIDS FOR DEVELOPING THE VOICE

In order to develop such a voice, constant practice in reading aloud will help. Good speech books will provide ample material in which a variety of attitudes and meanings are represented. Reading in a positive spirited manner will awaken responses to the intended meanings and help to develop interpretation skills.

Of equal importance is the need for listening to tones of other voices; particularly public speakers, radio announcers and actors. This will help one to become more aware of differences in time, pitch, volume, emphasis, and quality. Every speaker, as far as he is able, should attempt to develop a sense of tone discrimination.

One should develop a consciousness for his own voice. He should learn to respond to its changes in pitch and quality. Periodic voice recordings will be the greatest aid in learning the peculiarities and qualities of one's voice.

Finally, to eliminate vocal monotony and to have variety in expression, one must develop a flexible responsive vocal mechanism. The voice must be brought under control and capably express one's thoughts and feelings. This may be accomplished through an awareness of vocal effectiveness, by voice drills and exercises to achieve flexibility and control of the whole vocal mechanism, and through ear training for discrimination. Also constant practice in voicing such techniques as rate, duration, stress, pitch, inflection, emphasis, and others, which are basic in all speech training.

One should strive to develop a discriminating mind, a sensitive outlook toward the world which enables him to think in terms of speech concepts which are ideas and feelings and not mere words. He must learn to think discriminatingly while he is speaking in terms of these fuller concepts and feelings.

To support and complement this, so as to give a quality of vitality and personality to speech, one should endeavor to quicken his imagination to help arouse emotional responses.

CHAPTER FOUR

Stories for Chairmen—Some Comments for Chairmen

Full well they laughed with counterfeited glee
At all his jokes, for many a joke had he;

—Goldsmith

THE SPEECH CHAIRMAN AND THE HUMOROUS STORY

Most laymen, who are not experienced in serving as a program chairman, assume in order to be effective, that they must be funny; and to be funny they must tell many humorous stories.

As previously indicated, it is not to be assumed that the chairman or master-of-ceremonies should refrain completely from using stories. The important consideration in respect to their use, and which bears repeating, is, *what is the motive for using stories?* To be funny as an end in itself cannot but serve to detract from the purpose of the program as a whole.

A speaking program is designed solely to give an audience an opportunity to hear the message of a speaker. If a chairman loses sight of his relation in this definite purpose and obviously projects himself, the tail will wag the dog and the true purpose of the program is seriously affected.

THE BUSINESS OF THE CHAIRMAN

Fundamentally the main business of a chairman is to direct, guide and control the speaking program. He administers it. Strictly speaking and yet not paradoxically, the chairman is not *a part* of the actual speaking program, but rather a thing *apart from it*. He guides it best by not making himself too prominent; by not projecting himself to a point where he is more important than the speaker or speakers.

If there is only one speaker on a program, he will suffer immeasurably, if the chairman, by what he says or through his general demeanor, occupies too important a place. The chairman should not steal the spotlight from the speaker. He may occupy too important a place if he thinks it is his business to stand up and entertain the audience with stories which serve no purpose.

NEVER EMBARRASS THE SPEAKER

In fact, it is the chairman's job to make it easy for the speaker and to make him feel at ease before and during the time he speaks. The chairman should say or do nothing when he introduces a speaker which may detract from his speech or in any way embarrass him. If the speaker, before he begins, can sense the good will of the chairman, it will be of immeasurable aid to him. Too often a chairman, in a desire to be funny, engages in anecdotes about the speaker which verge on the personal, are irrelevant, and certainly not in good taste. As a result the speaker may be ill at ease and the quality of his speaking may be affected.

Some chairmen inadvertently say things or tell stories when introducing a speaker not intended to cause embarrassment, but they very often do, and more often cause a laugh to be directed at the chairman himself, thereby aiding the speaker.

A STORY WHICH IS A CLASSICAL EXAMPLE

Here is a story which may be used by an alert chairman. It is about the younger Joe Chamberlain, famous British statesman, whose speaking ability in Parliament brought praise from the great Gladstone.

Mr. Chamberlain was the speaker and guest of honor at a dinner in an important English city. The lord-mayor presided. At the end of the dinner coffee was being served and the guests were informally chatting and visiting with each other. The lord-mayor leaned over and touched Chamberlain, saying, "Shall we let the people enjoy themselves a little longer, or should we have your speech now?"

A TAILOR-MADE STORY FOR INTRODUCTIONS

Here is another excellent story which may be used when introducing speakers, particularly those small in stature.

When people remarked about the limited height of the early American colonist, Captain John Smith, he used to reply, "Small chimneys are easily fired." And this applied to the British-Welsh statesman, Lloyd George.

The British Chancellor was addressing a meeting in South Wales and the chairman when introducing him, trying to be funny at Lloyd George's expense, commented to the audience that he was a little disappointed in the statesman's physical appearance. He said:

"I had heard so much about Mr. Lloyd George that I naturally expected him to be a big man in every way; but, as you can see for yourselves, he is very small in stature."

Many a speaker would have been upset by such an introduction, but not Lloyd George.

When he responded he said, "I am disturbed that your chairman is disappointed in my size, but this is due to the way you have of measuring a man here. In North Wales we measure a man from his chin up, but you evidently measure him from his chin down."

Any chairman with an ounce of ingenuity may use this story when introducing a speaker of reasonable reputation so he may feel complimented rather than disturbed as he begins his speech.

SEVERAL ANECDOTES FOR CHAIRMEN

A chairman who is wise in the ways of proper procedure may impress the audience by using one of these little stories and give it confidence that he will not misuse the opportunity.

An example of the chairman overdoing, when introducing a speaker, is found in the recent situation when a prominent woman speaker had to sit and wait until the chairman engaged in a long harangue about her accomplishments and personality which was not especially appropriate. As she finally arose to speak she amusingly remarked, "After all the glowing remarks by the chairman, I could hardly wait to hear myself."

Cornelia Otis Skinner, the prominent actress, recently appeared as a guest star on a radio program. The person who introduced her engaged in flattering remarks. In the case of such a well-known artist as this lady, certainly "good wine needs no bush."

When she responded she felt the urge to remove the stigma of such an unnecessary introduction and she said, "Oh, oh, I'm here the wrong night again. This fellow certainly doesn't mean me."

Some speakers are not as courteous and subtle when they have to wait on a long-winded toastmaster. Perhaps a little on the facetious side is this story which is a good illustration!

The toastmaster insisted on making a speech. Then he thought it necessary to introduce two or three prominent citizens and each of these indulged in extended remarks without purpose. Finally, with the audience tired and the hour late, the speaker who had been engaged for the principal address was introduced. The toastmaster took it upon himself to make a long-winded introduction, and concluded by saying, "We will now have the address of the distinguished gentleman."

The speaker arose and said: "My address is 1170 Delaware Avenue. Good night."

SOME GUIDES FOR THE CHAIRMAN IN THE USE OF A STORY

If a story is not irrelevant to the speeches or program generally, and may appropriately aid the introductions, it has value.

If, however, it affects the mood or even tenor of the program by not being in harmony with it, it should not be used, no matter how well it may be rated as a story.

If the use of a story unduly prolongs the length of the program and digresses from the main purpose of the occasion, it should not be used. Even though it may be a proved laugh-getter, it may not be appropriate.

If it has any stigma of the personal, and may embarrass a speaker about to be introduced, it should not be used.

What has been said here about the use of the story aptly applies in spirit to general remarks made by the chairman.

YOU DON'T HAVE TO TELL STORIES

In place of the conventional humorous story which a speaker or chairman may not have on tap for a particular speech, this one may be used.

In her book *Memories*, Ethel Barrymore tells of a luncheon at the White House with President and Mrs. Coolidge. "Saw your brother John the other night in "Hamlet," Mr. Coolidge said. "He made a speech between the acts, told some very funny stories. That's a good way to make speeches, funny stories. I know some funny stories, but I think the American public likes to think of their President as being a sort of solemn ass and I think I'll just go on being a solemn ass."

The speaker may then add: "According to the philosophy of silent Cal Coolidge, a speaker is an ass if he doesn't tell funny stories, and, of course, this could well apply to the master-of-ceremonies. So tonight I have elected to be an ass. I am not going to tell stories."

A STORY FOR A CHAIRMAN INCLINED TO APOLOGIZE

Some comments will be made later about speakers who accept speaking engagements and then devote the greater part of their opening remarks apologizing for being the speaker. These comments will apply to chairmen who indulge in the same practice.

If a chairman feels inclined to say something about any inadequate feeling he may have in serving as a master-of-ceremonies, he had better do it in a spirit of humor. Certainly this will be a saving grace, whereas an apology will completely depreciate his value on a program. Here is a story with purpose, which may be used:

The following story from New England about a good chairman has especial value. This story may not be intended for use by a chairman or master-of-ceremonies although with the modification of the last line, as indicated below, it may be very effectively used by either. The story in its original form is designed for use by a speaker, who may, after having had what seems like a particularly good introduction, use it to respond to the chairman. Its use may be determined by the situation or occasion.

In a small New England city the community fund campaign had just gone over the top. The secretary of the campaign, a prim, gray-haired little lady, was called upon to say a few words about the chairman, a Mr. Smith, at a victory dinner.

"Ladies and gentlemen," she said, "in China there is an ancient custom that parents must kiss their offspring on that part of the anatomy through which they hope the children will become famous. If they want their child to be an orator, they kiss him on his mouth. If they hope he'll be a singer, they kiss him on the throat. Now I don't know on what part of his anatomy Mr. Smith's parents kissed him—" she paused an instant for effect—"but he certainly makes a wonderful chairman."

If a chairman of a speaking program wishes to use the story, the last line could be changed to read: "Now I am not sure my parents kissed me on the proper part of my anatomy, as I may not be a very good chairman."*

ONE FROM WILL ROGERS

The great American comedian and humorist, Will Rogers, once remarked, "I have spoken at so many banquets during the past few years that when I get home I feel disappointed if my wife and children don't get up and say, 'We have with us this evening a man whom, I am sure, needs no introduction.' "

The chairman in introducing a speaker who is reasonably well-known by an audience may use the last line of this anecdote by adding, "Ladies and gentlemen, I am standing up to say that this will serve to introduce our speaker, 'We have with us this evening a man whom, I am sure, needs no introduction, Mr. —————.' "

AUDIENCES DO EXPECT TO HEAR STORIES

Out of fairness to the chairman or master-of-ceremonies it may be said that audiences too often expect when he gets to his feet that the first thing he should do is to tell some humorous stories. The tendency is to associate humor with the chairman with little thought of associating it with the

*Adapted from Reader's Digest.

purpose of his remarks, or the introductions he is to make. American audiences want to be entertained. The great practice is to tell a gag and to make a joke.

A chairman, often sensing this psychological pressure of audiences, gives in too easily, and as a result commits the heinous faults of chairmen already cited. If he must succumb to this influence, he must do it with finesse or better yet with an indication that he is not completely out of step with his job, but is willing to humor them in their whims.

It will save him from the scorn of the judicious-minded, whose opinion according to Shakespeare "o'erweigh a whole theater of others."

A SPEAKER WHO WAS ABLE TO DO THIS

I recently heard Dr. You Chan Yang, the Ambassador to the United States from Korea, speak. He followed two other speakers, in addition to interspersing remarks by the chairman. Among them some stories had been indulged in, and when he began his remarks, he made special reference to the fact that the audience enjoyed the stories told.

He further commented that since he had come to the United States he had learned Americans expected speakers to tell stories. He said he thought he would begin by telling a story, just for the sake of telling a story, and it might heighten the good-will of a Korean speaker with an American audience, since it happened to a Korean young lady who came to the United States. If it does not seem appropriate or seems to be dragged in, he continued, "you may skin me alive," as the point of the story suggests.

Actually he didn't need to explain the reason for bringing in the story, because he was such an excellent speaker he was able to weave in a story very subtly.

THE STORY HE TOLD — WHICH CAN BE USED

A Korean young lady was being taught English by missionaries in preparation for her coming to America to complete her education. As a result she hadn't mastered the language completely and wasn't in control of some words and expressions.

She came to America and arrived at San Francisco for her initial stay. She was much impressed with the young ladies and women of the city and, in particular, their attractive faces and complexions.

She was expressing her delight with their appearance to a group of ladies at a gathering and she said, "You are beautiful; you have such beautiful hide."

One of the women sensing her meaning said, "We do not say hide, we say skin—you mean beautiful skin."

In her embarrassment, to make amends, she went off to a chapel and knelt down and prayed, "Skin me, oh my Savior skin me."   _____

A definition — A chairman is a man who spends most of the time which belongs to the speaker telling stories and then continues to use more of that time introducing the speaker, who needs no introduction.

A GOOD OPENING ANECDOTE TO BE USED
BY CHAIRMEN

When Al Smith, the one-time Democrat presidential nominee was governor of New York State, he was asked to speak to the inmates of a penitentiary in the Empire State.

He opened his remarks by addressing his audience: "Fellow-citizens," which brought a broad smile to the faces of his listeners.

He then added, "Friends and countrymen," which provoked general laughter in the audience.

Not to be daunted Al continued and said, "I'm glad to see so many of you here."

A chairman or speaker may use this story to good advantage for opening remarks by adding: You are not inmates in the sense that the members of Al Smith's audience were, and I hope you will not be sufferers, but, "I am happy to see so many of you here."

It seems many speakers and toastmasters have never learned not to consume fifteen minutes to make a five-minute speech.

A FAMOUS ACTOR LEARNED THE REASON

A stutterer once met the famous comedian, Nat Goodwin, and asked, "Mr. Goodwin, c-c-can you g-g-give m-m-me fifteen m-m-minutes of y-y-your time?"

"Certainly," replied Mr. Goodwin. "What is it you want?"

"I want to have a f-f-five minute's conversation w-w-with you."

SLIPS OF THE TONGUE BY SPEECH CHAIRMEN

John Mason Brown, author and drama critic, is one of America's most erudite and inspirational lecturers. He observes, as many speakers do about their names, that even though Brown is an easy name to remember—it could not be easier unless it were Smith or Jones—he has been introduced as almost everyone except Eleanor Roosevelt and Dorothy Thompson.

In his book *Accustomed As I Am,* he says . . . "my face used to fall, almost as the collective hopes of the audience would rise, when after hearing all the preliminaries, the chairman would graciously turn toward me, arm extended, and say, 'Ladies and gentlemen, it is with great pleasure that I introduce to you tonight, Mr. Heywood Brown.' "

But he claims this sort of thing is not the only example of the occupational disease known as "chairman's inspiration." The slips can be many and various and for them, he claims, only those who have never done any public speaking would dream of holding the chairman responsible.

A CONFUSED LADY INTRODUCER

Mr. Brown tells the story of a charming lady, who had won a gold pencil from Dale Carnegie and was introducing at a luncheon at which he spoke, an actor who had toured the previous season in the Skinner revival of *Candida.* "Ladies," she said, her eyes sparkling and her voice healthy with excitement, "it gives me great pleasure to present to you Mr. John Cromwell, who as you know, spent last winter traveling with Cornelia Otis Skinner in Canada."

A CHAIRMAN WHO NEVER PREPARED

On one speaking occasion Mr. Brown sat at dinner, prior to his lecture, with the gentleman who was to introduce him.

He saw Mr. Brown scribbling notes on the menu and he told him to relax. "Stop worrying about what you are going to say, relax. I don't believe in preparing speeches. Nope— preparation's no good. Spoils the charm of the thing; kills the gaiety. I just wait for the inspiration to come to me when I'm on my feet—and it never fails."

COURAGE MOUNTETH WITH OCCASION

He apparently believed as Shakespeare does that "courage mounteth with occasion," but here is an example of the inspiration he received, when he arose.

After several minutes of waiting, which his inspiration didn't interrupt, he gained the silence he desired. "Gentlemen," he said, "we have bad news for you tonight. We wanted to have Isaac F. Marcosson speak to you, but he couldn't come. He's sick. (applause.) Next we asked Senator Bledridge to address you on 'Migratory Workers,' but he was busy. (Applause.) Finally we tried in vain to get Doctor Lloyd Grogan of Kansas City to come down and speak to you about syphilis. (Applause.) So instead, we have—John Mason Brown." (Silence.)

The eminent Mr. Brown observes that the dislocations of the tongue and memory among those who introduce is that many of them lead very active lives. Often, of course, they are pinch-hitting for a previously designated chairman who has managed to leave town before the fateful evening. According to him, "hundreds of obliging relatives have been known to die just in time to make these precipitous exits possible." Usually, "the substitutes who replace these vanishing Americans frequently are apt to be no less busy than the men and women they serve as stand-ins."

Finally when you are seated in the chairs on the platform you first hear the report of the membership committee. "Whereupon a mild-voiced little lady stands up in the middle of the audience to say that due to the poor quality of the lecturers this year the membership has fallen off badly, and earnestly recommends a much better program for the coming season."

And then follows the finance committee's report. "At this point a lady or a gentleman gets up to say that the organization is not doing so well because of all the money they have had to pay to speakers. The audience applauds this vigorously, while you begin to wonder how many years you would get off for good behavior if you were sent up as an embezzler."

Then, the pre-occupied introducer gets to his feet with a special clearing of the throat which means your time has arrived.

You recognize he is holding in his hand the circular which your manager has sent on ahead and you have high hopes he will not indulge in a run down of your background, which it contains.

He has apparently forgotten why he has it and after a few ill-chosen remarks about the poor attendance being due to other things taking place he begins:

"As you all know, we have with us tonight, we have with us tonight a man who was born—well, that really doesn't matter, does it?—at any rate, he has been living—in Boston —no, New York since then. He is—uh—uh—a theatre editor and has written books which I am sure all you have read. Perhaps Mr. Mason—uh—uh—Brown will tell us more about himself. His subject is—well, he will probably announce that, too. Mr. Mason."

THE MORAL IS CLEAR

These anecdotes, culled and adapted in part from John Mason Brown's book "Accustomed As I Am," should point up a most essential moral for the speech chairman. If they don't, he should be happy in his ignorance and negligence and make speakers unhappy.

FINAL SUGGESTIONS FOR THE CHAIRMAN — KNOW THE SPEAKER

The most important duties of the chairman is to get acquainted with every speaker on the program and know something about them. He will be better able to do the job if he knows the speakers in advance of the speaking occasion and has a friendly and goodwill attitude toward them. If the right man is chosen for the job it is almost axiomatic that he will serve better if he knows something about the speakers. Besides getting acquainted with them, the chairman should manifest an interest in the speakers, and in a friendly, deft manner learn whatever he can about their background which may be useful to him in making the introductions. This has an important bearing on the next point.

DON'T HAVE TOO MUCH TO SAY

Aside from indulging in some levity to create a good mood and put the audience and speakers at ease, the chairman needs only to reveal the speaker's name, possibly a few facts about him, and briefly, if at all, his qualifications as a speaker, and the subject on which he is to speak. If he presents these in a clear and interesting manner, without garbling any of the details, he is rendering the program a valuable service. The important thing he must remember is to be brief; the chairman is not making the speech. He must not give his own views on the subject. He can emphasize the importance of the speaker's subject, if necessary, and how it applies to the audience. He should not talk about himself, or indulge in anecdotes about himself, or refer to his experience as a speaker.

DON'T USE HACKNEYED OR TRITE EXPRESSIONS

A speaker who uses the cliché, "Unaccustomed as I am to public speaking," should be boiled in oil. The chairman who, when introducing speakers, employs such trite expressions as, "We have with us tonight," or "It gives me great pleasure to introduce to you," deserves similar treatment. He should avoid the trite and over-used expression in the presentation.

And it is well to point out, don't constantly address the audience as "Ladies and Gentlemen." On formal occasions it may be all right, but this form becomes tiresome. Use your imagination and ingenuity.

When the speaker has finished, some expression of appreciation for his effort should be made and a brief allusion to the valuable and impressive parts of his speech. The use of a pause to serve as a transition before introducing the next speaker is essential.

ATTRIBUTES OF A GOOD CHAIRMAN

The chairman or master-of-ceremonies must be the master of the situation. He must know the people and the purposes of the occasion. It is not advisable to entrust the job to a stranger.

He should acquaint himself with the program; know who is going to speak, or who is going to entertain. He should know each speaker's subject and the name of each entertainer's number or contribution. He should conceive and understand the function of each part of the program and its relation to the whole.

He should know how to speak little and yet say much. But he should prepare his opening and later remarks, even though it is expected he may have to modify these according to the trend or turn of events.

He should refrain from telling too many funny stories, even though he may be expected to be humorous and make apt introductions.

He should prepare a time schedule. He should know how long the program or meeting should last and apportion to each person his allotted time. He should, before the meeting, tell each of them how much time is at his disposal.

He must be on time and see that members of the program are likewise. He must start the meeting on time and then keep things moving on schedule as nearly as possible.

He must strive to be alert, alive, and resourceful. If he can, with other things being equal, possess wit and humor, he will make an exceptional chairman.

It is recognized, therefore, that he has autocratic power.

He has the first and the last word. With it, he must possess tact.

He must, as a final admonition, never overdo; for overdoing has a tendency to "steal the thunder" of other speakers.

A writer in discussing echoes of the Hollywood Academy Awards of a few years back brings something pertinent to our ideas:

"Robert Montgomery was the best master-of-ceremonies we've ever had. He must get credit for his excellent management and pace of the program. He was witty, right to the point, and didn't try to give a performance for himself. I vote for him as the master-of-ceremonies next year."

In his lines on "The Toastmaster," James Metcalfe, with some misgivings, admirably expresses what may be the poor

chairman's fate. The poetry is not very good, but the ideas
are.

"The Toastmaster"

He is the banquet boss whose job
Is not an easy one,
Because he has to guide the course,
Of business and of fun;
He introduces speakers in
A pleasant sort of way,
And gives a little hint or two
Of what they are to say.
He calls attention to the guests,
And tells a joke or two,
And he must have the parting word,
When all the rest are through.
Sometimes this kind of creature knows
Precisely when to pause,
And how to hold the audience
And draw the most applause;
But sometimes he is not so hot,
Or does not know the score;
And by his smart or clumsy style
Turns out to be a bore.

Considering the high importance of the position of chairman, an authority in a former day once said, "To be a good
chairman, is to be greater than a king." The thought may
suggest exaggeration, but it carries the idea that a good
chairman is rare, indeed.

CHAPTER FIVE

Stories About Speakers for Speakers—
Some Speech Principles

"'Twas the saying of an ancient sage, that humour was the only test of gravity, and gravity of humour. For a subject which would not bear raillery was suspicious; and a test which would not bear a serious examination was certainly false wit."—Shaftesbury

Humorous stories contained in this volume are designed for use by speakers and chairmen. But strangely enough, some of the best stories and most amusing anecdotes concern the characteristics and peculiarities of speakers and emcees.

Here are included a group of stories which are based upon these peculiarities, and the speech practices or habits of many chairmen and speakers. Even though these stories serve to point up the humorous aspects of the faults of speakers, they contain for the most part a serious and additional purpose. And, of course, this is an interesting and logical basis for all humorous stories. Bing Crosby says, "You know, the greatest basis for comedy is a serious undertone in the story." And Bob Hope recognizing the importance of this psychology says, "I try to start with a serious background and work comedy out of it. It's a successful formula." In this respect, the stories, through humor, reveal practices which are contrary to effective speech, and ridicule the human tendencies of speakers who are guilty of these speaking misdemeanors.

Actually no speaker should be unaware of the evil ways which speakers fall upon. If he is not aware of them, and by absence or lack of technique becomes guilty himself, he may in time be rudely awakened by his audiences.

The truth is that audiences know only too well the unfortunate practices of speakers. They constantly have misgivings that each new speaker may be a party to them. They are, therefore, pleased to have any expression from a speaker who shows his disdain for such shortcomings; and they like speakers who can treat them in a humorous way, by using good stories which poke fun at imaginary and actual speakers who are guilty of practices which disturb and are unfair to audiences.

REASONS FOR USING SUCH STORIES

The use of such stories should give the audience reasonable assurance that the speaker will not be an offender; that he has a sure sense of speech values which should make him worth listening to; and if the stories contain humor he will be an added attraction.

For these reasons alone, no speaker should be considered truly developed as a speaker who fails to recognize the importance for using stories of the type which follow. They are highly essential to his success, and serve as an indispensable aid.

PARTICULAR PURPOSES AND VALUES OF STORIES

The special value and appeal of these stories lie in their ability to point out particular weaknesses and virtues of those who speak. They include stories about speakers who are long-winded and can't end a speech; those who speak when they have nothing to say; and those who accept speaking engagements and spend all their time apologizing for doing so. They also include amusing accounts about speech chairmen who are guilty of equally vicious habits.

Conversely, some of the anecdotes concern the virtues of those who appear before audiences. Speakers, who when called upon, say the appropriate thing; and those who have the knack or faculty of adapting a story to a special need or occasion.

It can be repeated that the principles and the ideas they treat about speakers, with the added commentary included in these pages, are the "sine qua non" of those who would be wise and well-rounded speakers. It is, therefore, to be assumed that this chapter constitutes an important part of the book.

THE SPEAKER ALWAYS HAS AN AUDIENCE

It is important for the speaker to remember that he always has an audience of various types of individuals. If he entertains any doubts about members of his audience being interested in his subject or what he is saying, it seems almost axiomatic that in every audience there are those who are interested in him as a public speaker.

According to the accepted theory in public speaking the audience is interested in you as the speaker on a purely curiosity basis or a "show us what you've got" attitude until you say something, and then it is interested in what you are saying and how you are saying it. If you have nothing to say, its interest for the most part ends or subsides. Between that initial interest in you and the interest in your speech, when you begin it, is what is known in public speaking as the deadline of interest.

There are some few listeners whose interest is largely in the speaker by virtue of his speaking techniques, and they measure his effectiveness in terms of his presentation of subject matter rather than the subject matter alone. This is, as it should be in every speaker-audience situation. Of course, it is reasonable to assume a speaker can't have good speech techniques without good speech content, and conversely the speech content is seriously affected by the presence or lack of proper techniques.

Some listeners, though perhaps in the minority, may study and show concern for poor techniques exhibited by a speaker and may even be sympathetic toward any resulting ineffectiveness on his part. This, strangely enough, is what constitutes vicarious appreciation; suffering with the speaker who doesn't do well because they sometime may be in the same position. It can, of course, work in the opposite way for listeners so sensitively constituted. They can revel with the speaker, who by virtue of fine techniques, does a good job. In the last analysis, vicarious appreciation of what speakers do constitutes a reliable basis for critical opinion.

As the speaker in the following story, there may be some interested in your speaking, even though others aren't, because they are potential speakers and have a real vicarious interest.

A SYMPATHETIC SPEAKER

The speaker began his speech before a full audience. People gradually kept getting up and leaving until no one remained but one person. The speaker continued to talk and the one person listening to him remained until he had finished his speech. The speaker then thanked him for his courtesy in remaining to listen to him for it gave him an audience of one anyhow.

The remaining person replied, "Oh I'm not a member of your audience. I'm the next speaker."

THE PHYSICAL BASIS OF SPEECH

We have a story here which can be used to point up the importance of the physical aspect of speech. But first, a few comments.

Some speakers may believe that all speaking to an audience is done by word of mouth or actual speaking. The connotation of the word *audience* doesn't mean those who only listen. The truth is an audience doesn't receive the speaker's full message through what it hears alone or by the auditory senses, but if the listeners of any audience are alert and intent upon getting the full meaning of that message they must react with several other senses. This is necessary if the true communicative process is to prevail and if there is to be rapport with the speaker.

A SPEAKER IS MORE THAN SOMEONE TO BE HEARD

There is a speech axiom which says that *a man speaking is a thing to be heard, a thing to be seen, thereby carrying a message to others.* So it is not by word of mouth alone by which the speaker communicates. And it is true in the history of the race and with the individual that communication is pantomime first.

Every accomplished speaker or actor knows the body is a most effective agent or medium of communication and he strives to employ the specialized parts of the body such as the hands, the arms, the torso, the head, and the face to augment and vivify the spoken word. A good speaker could not operate if he were denied the use of his physical parts in getting his message across. He would be like a boxer with his hands tied behind him.

It was the late Edward Arnold, the actor, upon being asked by a young actor what to do to improve his art told him, "learn to fill the pauses." He meant, of course, to fill the silences between the spoken words with effective pantomime and action; known in the acting art as employing effective pantomimic transitions. He could have well added, "learn to interpret or communicate by actions as well as words."

In her book "How to Make a Speech Before Secondary School Students," published recently by the National Sales Executive's Press of New York, Julia O'Meara, a former student of the writer, and a successful teacher of student and adult speakers endorses the importance of the physical aspect in speech.

Using as her prime thesis that, *A Speaker Must Know His Audience*, Miss O'Meara says, "From the moment *she sees* a speaker take the platform, she knows whether or not he will hold his audience." And then she reveals that the physical demeanor is the key to her knowing by adding, "A talk before an audience is not delivered with the mouth alone. It demands the whole body. That is why, at the conclusion, a speaker can be as tired as a football player after a game."

If the audience is to get the full message of the speaker it will complement what it hears with what it sees. The interpreter or speaker who challenges the visual as well as the auditory sense will heighten the value of his message.

SUIT THE ACTION TO THE WORD . . .

But with it all, the speaker must learn the secret of the proper use of the body, gestures and facial expression. If there is a lack of coordination of the body with the spoken word, the designed purpose of aiding or improving communication is defeated, or seriously affected. Practice is essential for those who do not instinctively coordinate action with speech and speech with action. As Shakespeare says, "suit the action to the word, the word to the action."

A STORY WHICH HAS SPEECH VALUES

In teaching public speaking the observation is often made that too many people make speeches because *they want to say something, rather than because they have something to say.*

This story points up the important speech principle that it is wise not to talk if you have nothing of importance to say. The story in its original form is credited to Leonard Lyons from his "Lyons Den" column.

It also serves as a good example of a speaker's ability to adapt a story to a particular occasion or need, which is discussed in the opening chapter of this volume as an important or necessary technique if one is to be a successful storyteller.

The story was told recently by a college professor who was invited to give an entertaining talk at the banquet of a college sorority.

When the professor was introduced he arose, acknowledged the introduction, and said, "As I stand before you to begin my remarks, a story about Albert Einstein comes to my mind.

"Dr. Frank Aydelotte, president of Swarthmore College, once invited Albert Einstein to be guest of honor at a dinner. When Einstein was introduced as the speaker he said: 'Ladies and gentlemen, I'm sorry but I have nothing to say.'

"Then he sat down. Surprised by this announcement the guests immediately started buzzing. Upon hearing it Einstein arose again and added: 'In case I do have something to say, I'll come back.'

"Six months later he wired President Aydelotte: 'Now I have something to say.' Aydelotte immediately arranged another dinner, when according to the story, Einstein made a good speech.

"Now," continued the professor, "I feel very much in the mood of Professor Einstein. Last year you invited me as a guest to this fine banquet. I had a good dinner and then I gave a talk which you seemed to appreciate. I thoroughly enjoyed myself. Here I am as a guest tonight. I've had a splendid dinner and I've enjoyed myself again. What I'm worrying about is next year. If I give a talk now, how can I manage next year to be at this fine affair?

"It occurred to me, if I used the Einstein formula, I could say, I have nothing to say, but I shall be glad to come back when I do. I could arrange to get in touch with you just before the affair next year and then advise you: I now have something to say."

The girls at the banquet had a good laugh and the last I heard, they had promised to invite the professor next year for their annual banquet.

DON'T MAKE A SPEECH JUST BECAUSE YOU'RE CALLED ON

A college president I know was called on by a chairman to say a few words. Upon responding he said he was reminded of a story which seemed appropriate.

"During a recent ocean voyage, a storm blew up and a young woman, leaning against the rail, lost her balance and was thrown overboard into the rough sea.

Before the ship could be halted, another figure plunged overboard into the water beside her.

To the astonishment of everyone, it was the oldest man on the cruise—an octogenarian. He held the girl above the water until a lifeboat picked them up.

That evening the old man was given a party in recognition of his bravery. "Speech! Speech!" cried everyone enthusiastically.

The old gentleman rose and looked around the gathering

carefully. "I have just one thing to ask," he said testily. "Who pushed me?"

The college president said, "I am not asking who pushed me into this vertical position. I am merely saying, don't push me into making a speech. I paid my way to this affair, which entitles me to hear someone else speak, not to hear myself. I am happy to be here." He sat down. He made an impression.

BE HUMOROUS ABOUT THE SERIOUS

A speaker can often indicate to the audience that he has a full awareness of the importance of the time element in respect to his remarks by the use of the anecdote or story about speakers or speeches that are dull because they are too long. He can, if he is careful not to make his own speech too long, use humor to good advantage with his audience.

The writer has always found that stories about speakers who encounter audience difficulties as a result of speaking too long are always enjoyed. The reason is obvious. There is a basic psychology involved which concerns every audience; it touches their welfare and they are ready to laugh about speakers who take advantage of them. And as is pointed out in the introductory remarks of this section, much successful humor is based on a serious background.

A SPEAKER IN TEXAS WHO COULDN'T END HIS SPEECH

In a town deep in the heart of Texas a visiting speaker had noticed with slight concern when he was introduced to his audience that some of its stalwart members carried holsters with guns. The fact made no impression upon him when he got to talking. He spoke forty minutes, fifty minutes, and continued beyond an hour. It was then, however, that the gun-toting members in the audience had a singular and frightening effect upon him; heretofore, they had given him only passing concern. He noticed they had removed their guns from the holsters and were pointing the business ends of them in his general direction.

With his complacency somewhat disturbed, he stopped his speaking and turned to the speech chairman, and asked if these men in the audience were "fixin' " to shoot him. The chairman said, "No, they're not fixin' to shoot you; they wouldn't be that discourteous; they're just fixin' to shoot the man who brought you."

DON'T APOLOGIZE—IT'S TOO LATE

The author has used this story:

A speaker who sensed he had spoken too long and had practically put his audience into a coma by his long drawn-out remarks tried to redeem himself by saying, "I'm sorry if I have gone beyond my time limit, but you see I didn't have my watch with me. A member of the audience remarked in tones audible enough to be heard, "No, but there's a calendar right behind you."

A wise speaker could add, "I don't intend to take too much time, and I have brought my watch."

A SPEAKER WHO FOLLOWED THE CALENDAR

A movie executive famous for making long after-dinner speeches suddenly became noted for his brevity. When asked about his reformation he replied: "It was a remark I overheard during a pause in one of my speeches. One man said to another, 'What follows this speaker?' And the other fellow replied, 'Wednesday.' "

IT ALSO HAPPENED IN MARK TWAIN'S DAY

Here again is a story which may be used by the chairman or the speaker.

Mark Twain, according to Milton Dickens, speech teacher at the University of Southern California, is credited with a story about an overlong sermon. At the end of twenty minutes he was so favorably impressed by the sermon he decided to put in five dollars when the offering was taken. Twenty minutes later, he decided that two dollars would suffice. After another twenty minutes the considered contribution shrank to one dollar. When eventually the sermon ended, Mark Twain was practically aroused from a sleep by the man with the offertory plate, and he responded by putting in a nickel.

A SPEAKER WHO LOST HIS AUDIENCE

The following story is credited to humorist, E. E. Kenyon.

A well-known speaker, much in demand today, admits he wasn't always so popular—and tells about one of his earlier speeches which would have discouraged anyone with less tenacity.

He was speaking before a large audience and he thought he was doing very well until he noticed the audience disappearing—one by one.

The room was nearly empty and the inexperienced man was trying vainly to find a way to cut his speech short when an usher handed him a note.

"When you are through," it read, "will you please turn off the lights, lock the doors and leave the key in the manager's office?"

NEVER APOLOGIZE

Some More Comments About This Cardinal Speech Principle

A speaker should always remember, the mere fact he is asked to participate in a program is an indication that the committee and the audience have confidence in his ability and expect him to do the job. He should rise to the occasion and attempt to meet the challenge. If he has confidence in his ability because of some experience, has an adequate background and has made the necessary preparation for the speech, he should assume the right attitude toward the job. If he has any misgivings about his ability, he should apply the psychology so aptly proposed by Shakespeare in *Hamlet,* "Assume a virtue if you have it not." He should never apologize for being the speaker. First, it is not in good form. And further, if he is any good the audience will find that out; if he is no good, the audience will find that out too without being told.

If he feels a necessity to say something about any feeling of humility he may have, or even a slight inadequateness (which should never be made known to the audience), he should do it in a spirit of levity to take the edge off the effect produced by apologizing.

In place of the vicious apology for making a speech, too often indulged in by speakers, who immediately depreciate their own value, it is suggested that a good story be used at the outset.

A STORY THE SPEAKER MAY USE IN PLACE OF THE PROVERBIAL APOLOGY

A young boy had been going to the cellar where a large barrel of molasses was stored. He was in the habit of running his fingers on parts of the barrel to get drippings of the molasses. One day to his surprise he found the top removed from the barrel and upon investigating and finding it half full, he either fell in or decided to get in the barrel. He stuck his head out over the top and was heard to say in a prayer-like manner, "Oh, Lord, make my tongue equal to this opportunity."

Of course, this is the fervent prayer or hope of every speaker.

THAT UNEXPECTED TALK

It is an unwise and unfair chairman who calls on a person to speak without warning him in advance and who expects an adequate response. Likewise, it is only a novice in the field of speaking who is present at a speech occasion, and who occupies an important place in relation to the program, who really anticipates being called on and does nothing about it. The truth is that the experienced chairman knows in advance whom he is going to call on and informs the speaker. Conversely, the experienced speaker anticipates the possibility of being called on. So let it be set down as fundamental, that in the realm of public speaking there are few speakers called on unexpectedly, and, therefore, the typical impromptu speech is a rarity.

Further remarks on this subject, delivered over twenty years ago in a radio speech by Mr. Henry Roberts, a speech teacher, are still of interest. They have been repeated enough to have become a classic and are in no way trite, unless the Twenty-Third Psalm is trite. Here they are in part: "Now, have you ever heard a polished after-dinner speaker . . . astound an audience . . . and who carefully left the impression that he had waited until after coffee had been served before giving the least thought to his remarks? You probably went away greatly impressed and not a little mystified at his uncanny ability to make a speech with little or no warning—what you called 'his ability to think on his feet.'

"In the first place, that brilliant impromptu speech of the polished after-dinner speaker probably wasn't impromptu at all. More likely, as Mark Twain says, it had 'been carefully prepared in private and tried on any appreciative object.' "

Most speakers who are capable of making effective impromptu speeches have had considerable experience in preparing them and are reasonably adept, when there is only a short time at their disposal to organize their thoughts to the best advantage. They have recognized, as one authority has observed, that while the occasion may be impromptu the thought doesn't have to be.

Here is a good example of a speaker who gave what seemed to be a good impromptu speech:

A GOOD RESPONSE—PREMEDITATED OR UNPREMEDITATED

"Don't Steal The Show" From The Main Speaker

Some years ago I attended the annual dinner of Buffalo's Gridiron Club. This organization is the counterpart of Washington's notable Gridiron Club. The annual affair of both groups is dedicated to the business of "giving the business" to well-known personalities, who are the targets for ridicule, and the buffoonery is at their expense.

On this particular occasion Joe McCarthy, the ex-major league baseball manager, whose home is in Buffalo, was the main speaker. It was the winter after he had been unceremoniously released as manager of the New York Yankees by the fireball, Larry MacPhail.

A young lawyer who was in Buffalo after a service stretch with the O. S. S. was one of an array of speakers called upon before McCarthy was introduced.

He knew of McCarthy's experience with MacPhail and the Yankees; he was also mindful of the number of people being called upon to speak, including himself. He began by saying:

"There have been a number of people called on to speak and now I am added to the array. As I am not the speaker I have a little story which I think is appropriate.

"Last year, 1946, was the year most of us came back from the service. In baseball it was said it was the year the men came back. Last spring our speaker here was managing the Yankees and he was awaiting the veterans and stars to return to replace the rookies and old-timers. Before he was able to use the new strength and bring a pennant to the Yankees, our friend Mr. Larry MacPhail upset the apple cart and Joe McCarthy resigned.

"Now on May 24th, the same MacPhail made a surprise move. He appointed Bill Dickey, the team's catcher, (recently a Yankee coach) to succeed McCarthy. No one ever thought of Bill as a manager. Possibly as a coach, when his catching days were over, but as a manager, no one had ever thought of that. No one, except MacPhail.

"Bill handled the team for a series in Boston and then the Yankees were at the Stadium.

"It was then a reporter approached Bill and said to him: 'Now that you've had at least a few days on the job, how does it feel to be a manager?'

"Bill paused and then answered slowly but honestly, 'Funny thing, I keep looking around for McCarthy.' "

The lawyer concluded by saying, "If Bill Dickey were here, he would still keep looking around for McCarthy. I understood McCarthy was going to be the speaker tonight. But I've heard everybody else except him, including myself. As Bill Dickey did, I keep looking around for McCarthy. McCarthy, where are you?"

He was a howling success and it got McCarthy off to a good start when he was introduced.

WHERE IS THE MAIN SPEAKER?

The above story very definitely raises the question, "Where is the main speaker?" Too often, in connection with speech programs and banquets, too many people other than the main speaker are called on to speak. If these people have any sense they will realize, when called upon, whether they have anything to contribute. If not they should not attempt to talk as they will encroach upon the time and importance of the main speaker. The above story has value on such occasions. Previous remarks have been made on this point, the importance of a talk and its relation to the program as a whole.

ANOTHER AUTHORITY'S OPINION ON THE UNEXPECTED TALK

Elizabeth Ferguson von Hesse, a prominent speech teacher, in her book *So To Speak*, has made this rather abrupt observation. "Never say, 'I did not expect to be called upon this evening.' You know, even though you had not been asked before . . . , you hoped you would get a chance to speak and that nearly everyone present secretly feels the same way."

This is true for most people, even though they are often sorry after they have been called upon.

A GOOD STORY TO OPEN A SPEECH

University of Michigan's famous football coach and its present director of athletics, Fritz Crisler, is a popular speaker on the banquet circuit. Crisler has the reputation for being a good storyteller and the following story is supposed to be from his repertoire.

This story has particular value for a speaker who wishes to open his speech on a note of levity instead of a vicious apology for being asked to speak, in which some speakers indulge. As is pointed out elsewhere on these pages, a speaker should NEVER APOLOGIZE; this is a cardinal principle in public speaking.

The Wolverine's coach had been asked to speak before a certain men's organization. Crisler made his usual careful preparation and upon completing the speech, judging from the response, he assumed he had done a pretty good job. The chairman of the occasion then approached him and handing him a ten-dollar check said, "Please accept this check as a small appreciation for your speech." Crisler declined, saying it wasn't necessary, but the chairman seemed insistent that he take it. Crisler again said no, saying he would prefer to have the organization keep it. The club member then agreed, "I'll put it in our fund," he said. The famous coach replied, "Oh, you have a fund? What is it for?" "To get better speakers," came back the quick reply of the chairman.

The speaker may with a few transitional remarks suggest that he hopes he satisfies, otherwise the group for whom he is speaking may be prompted to use such a fund, if it has one.

SOME GOOD RESPONSES

A speaker arose and said:

"The American institution of the banquet has been described by a well-known after-dinner speaker as 'an affair where a speaker first eats a lot of food he doesn't want, and then proceeds to talk about something he doesn't understand to a lot of people who don't want to hear him.'

"I heartily subscribe to this. I have eaten too much and I don't feel like talking, I don't want to say anything because I have nothing to say, and finally, I don't want to talk because I'm sure you don't want to listen to me.' "

When called on another speaker said:

"Gellett Burgess, eminent American humorist remarked: 'To sit and be pumped into is not an exhilarating process.' To which some quipster added, 'No matter how elaborate the pump.'

"I am certainly not an elaborate pump."

It is obvious that tennis alone is not the forte of Helen Wills Moody. It is reported that at a dinner celebrating athletic stars, the tennis star finally got to her feet at the end of a long program and won everybody's heart by saying:

"To be seen one must stand up—to be heard one must speak clearly—but to be appreciated one must sit down."

A good speaker is a fellow who says the things you would like to have thought of in the way you would like to have said them had you thought of them.

I heard one person respond, when called upon, with this definition of a speaker. He said, "the more good speakers

I hear, the more I am convinced that I am not one, because I can't do any of the things they do. I prefer, therefore, to let others do the speaking."

THE SPEECH PRELIMINARY

Before a speaker begins a speech or engages in the actual introduction, he should make some preliminary remarks. Aside from acknowledging the introduction and giving an expression of pleasure for being called upon or for being the speaker, he should respond to the particular remarks of the chairman. This is what is known as the preliminary part of the speech—and is quite aside from the introduction.

This response to the remarks of the chairman is really in the category of the unexpected or the impromptu and, depending upon the way it is given, can affect the whole impression made by a speaker.

It is the first impression made upon the audience, and it requires planning in the mind of the speaker if it is to be definitely impressed upon the audience. As one speech authority puts it, the beginning remarks of any speech must be "clear, compact and concrete."

Speakers who know their business always establish an immediate worthwhile impression by using carefully thought-out remarks in the beginning. Those who wish to attain audience acceptance should strive to do likewise. Very often the cue for making a good beginning may rest within the remarks of the chairman. Listen carefully to his remarks for such a cue and then attempt to build a novel response around it.

Here is a good example of a speaker taking the lead from the comments of the chairman to set up his preliminary response:

ACTOR ANTHONY QUINN RESPONDS TO
THE CHAIRMAN

It is reasonable to assume that this story is authentic. It is reported that at a recent Hollywood gathering Anthony Quinn, the movie actor, was welcomed after his return from Europe where he had been making some pictures. The chairman of the occasion referred to Quinn's work in the Italian pictures he had made and what an unusual privilege it was for him to play love scenes with those beautiful Italian actresses. And then he was called on to tell something about his trip to the continent and his picture-making experience.

He arose, and after acknowledging the welcome, he said: "I think it was Edward Robinson whom I once congratulated for his having played in a picture with the great Russian actress Ouspenskaya. 'Yes,' Robinson replied, 'it is true I appeared with Marie Ouspenskaya and I'm glad, because if I hadn't, I should never have known how to pronounce her name.'

"It is true I appeared in or made pictures with the leading Italian actresses of the screen. I played scenes with"— and then he hesitated—but promptly enthralled and amused his audience by naming in rapid-fire order and in clear perfect pronunciation, with his exotic quality, the names of the beautiful current cinema stars of Italy, who have caught the fancy and gained the admiration of the American public—"Anna Magnani, Gina Lollobrigida, Sylvano Mangano, Lea Padovani, Rosano Podesta." And then he added, "Of course I'm thrilled with the experience, and I know exactly what Edward Robinson meant, how else could I have learned to pronounce their names?"

He smiled and with easy transition entered upon the more prosaic parts of his speech.*

ANOTHER KIND OF INAPPROPRIATE SPEECH

It has just been observed that responses to introductions of a speaker which do not take into account what the chairman has said about the speaker are inappropriate and have a serious effect upon good speechmaking.

Equally bad is the practice of some speakers who engage in a display of words; who are deluded by the impression that effective speech is measured by the degree one can employ profound and obscure words. They may think the use of fancy and polysyllabic words is an indication of intelligence. This sort of profundity, however, has nothing to do with successful speechmaking because it obscures the ideas, if a speaker has any. May we remind all who would interest listeners and move audiences that the basic purpose and end and aim of all speaking is to communicate ideas. Successful speaking is primarily measured by that one criterion. Great speakers and great writers have pretty largely depended upon mono and duosyllabic words to get their thoughts across. The classic example of this is to be found in the writings and speeches of Abraham Lincoln. Read them, and read the writings of St. Paul, both masters of style or rhetoric, who never obscure their thoughts by words or stylish language.

ON PREPARING REMARKS IN ADVANCE

There are two types of individuals who appear on speaking programs, whom we shall not dignify by calling speakers —who are absolute bores.

* *The Master Guide For Speakers*, V. Spencer Goodreds.

First, there is the person who definitely expects to be called on to give a talk or make remarks at a gathering, and then responds in an indefinite vague manner, which has an unfortunate effect on the program, and says, "I did not expect to be called upon this evening." Because of his total inadequateness he usually continues by indulging in an unfortunate apology for not being prepared. Some people who call themselves speakers are guilty of this vicious habit.

Next, there is the person who also expects to be called upon and prepares his remarks or talk without regard to any appropriateness they may have for the occasion. The particular offender I have in mind is the one who plans an elaborate, flowery response to an imaginery build-up the chairman will give him when he is introduced. When the occasion arises the chairman merely introduces him as the speaker but, to the letter, he indulges in the response he has prepared, in which he imagined the chairman was singing his praises as an individual or a speaker. Such a practice, of course, is built upon a false illusion about the necessity of acknowledging the introduction with an elaborate response, with no regard for its appropriateness to what actually may be said. Some introductions require no response, and none requires predetermined comment based on anticipated or hoped-for remarks by the chairman. In any event the response should be guided and determined by what is actually said at the time of the introduction. It should not be overdone in thought and expression. It should be brief and always appropriate.

ALEXANDER WOOLLCOTT MUST CONTRIBUTE TO EVERY STORY COLLECTION

The appellation of raconteur should be reserved for only those who excel in the art of storytelling. The late Alexander

Woollcott justly deserved this title. For if ever there were a writer, and particularly a speaker, who knew the place for and the purpose of a story, it was he. His stories were always apropos and heightened the value of his remarks. He was a master in weaving a story into his talks with a deftness which was without parallel. His stories had a natural quality in themselves, and a natural appeal in their use.

I introduced him to a college audience once and while I don't remember what particularly occasioned a story he told, it has pointed value for all who engage in speechmaking. The story has to do with the use of gestures in speaking and points up the important principle that gestures must come naturally as a result of feeling and be coordinated with the expression; they cannot be dragged in for the mere purpose of using gestures. It must be, as Shakespeare proposes, a case of "action to suit the word. . . ." Modern speech recognizes the importance of having gestures in speaking come spontaneously and to spring from impulses, rather than being studied and according to rules.

In telling the story Woollcott was able to draw from the experiences of the happy days at his dear Hamilton College in Clinton, New York. The recollections of his alma mater are so fondly recounted in parts of his book "While Rome Burns."

It was the vogue when he was a student at Hamilton, and it may still be, that before a student could graduate he must, as a senior, give a speech before the assembled student body.

The senior speech or oration in Woollcott's day was the culmination of four years of training in public speaking, rhetoric and, in addition, the proper and necessary gestures for oratory.

The art of gesture was studied separately from speech composition. The gestures included, for example, the hands or hand supine, the hands prone, the hands averse, the hands vertical and the hands in various index positions, and the clenched fist. The gestures were applied to various parts of the speech, where they seemed to accentuate and point up the meaning.

Woollcott recounts that as a senior he had prepared his speech most carefully, and indicated at various places in the manuscript the use of this or that type of gesture as the necessary one to accentuate the spoken word or idea. He had practiced diligently and matched the gestures with the speech, with seeming smoothness.

He appeared before the assembled students for its delivery. He got started well and was going along swimmingly, speaking with conviction and using gestures with apparent ease and finesse. Somewhere through the speech, however, Woollcott's enthusiasm for what he was saying got beyond him and he neglected to use the accompanying gestures. He suddenly realized he was running out of words, but not so with gestures and he ended the speech with a goodly number of the gestures left over or unused. To make certain he would get credit for using all the gestures, he then engaged in a rapid succession of movements of the hands and arms, displaying the unused gestures in sign language fashion.

Woollcott, as he told the story, heightened its appeal by accompanying the explanation of the neglected gestures with effective pantomime.

The business "looked good on him." If properly done, it makes a good story.

SPEAKING OF GESTURES—A CATHOLIC BISHOP TELLS ONE

Bishop Joseph O'Shea of Philadelphia was telling a group of friends some time ago about a sermon he preached in St. Francis de Sales Church in the city of brotherly love.

The bishop said the service was exclusively for deaf mutes and that an interpreter stood beside him throughout and translated it in sign language. Commented the bishop:

"My sermon didn't sound so good, but it looked swell."

GESTURES FOR ANOTHER PURPOSE

A young clergyman just graduated from the theological seminary had been given his first church assignment. Not wishing to face the responsibility alone he acquired a bride.

On the occasion of his first service the young wife sat in the church balcony with definite instructions to watch carefully how her husband conducted himself and to pay particular attention to his sermon. He went through the early part of the service without difficulty, and then he entered the pulpit to begin the sermon. Before he actually began to preach he made a signal impression by raising his hands to the left side of his head with palms facing in; he lowered them and then began his sermon. As he reached the obvious conclusion of the sermon he engaged in the same business of raising his hands but on the right side of his head.

After the service he exchanged greetings with members of the congregation. They were gracious and all seemed pleased, and no one made reference to the unusual gestures he had used in the beginning and ending of his sermon.

When they had gone the young preacher immediately approached his wife to get the verdict on his efforts. He asked her expectantly and with considerable enthusiasm: "Well," he said, "how did I do?"

"Well, fine," she answered, but immediately added, "What was the idea of the gestures before and after your sermon?"

Without hesitating he replied, "Oh those, they were the quotation marks."

Franklin D. Roosevelt's advice to his son, James, on the subject of speechmaking was: "Be sincere; be brief; be seated."

CHAPTER SIX

Stories About Professors and Teachers

"I should but teach him how to tell my story." — Othello.

STORIES ABOUT PROFESSORS AND TEACHERS

As a college teacher for some years, I know there is no story of greater appeal to the college audience than that one which concerns the quirks and idiosyncracies of the college professor. College students are susceptible to such stories because they so well bespeak the antics and behavior patterns of their own teachers.

Stories about teachers generally have great interest; but the appeal of such stories goes beyond those who are still in the classroom. It is an appeal which is literally universal, because we all have been taught, and such stories recall with delight the teachers under whom we sat as students.

STORIES TO BE USED BY EDUCATORS AND OTHER SPEAKERS

Some of these stories grew out of actual situations. Others have been developed to point up typical or suggested classroom happenings and the peculiarities of teachers. These stories should find popular appeal for school audiences or among educators and when used by the teacher, professor, or student speaker.

Many of the stories may be used in their present form; others may be changed to suit occasions.

THE ABSENT-MINDED PROFESSOR

During the years I taught on the faculty of a New England college, I had an associate, a capable teacher, who because of his gracious kind manner and his ever-present smile, was known affectionately by the students as "Sunny Jim." For the purposes of the story, we shall call him "Sunny Jim" Holmes. Professor Holmes was profound, but he did on numerous occasions reveal the characteristic trait of many professors, "absent-mindedness."

On one particular morning the professor was driving alone up the street which approached the college campus. He stopped and picked up one of the students who was on his way to class. As they drove along they engaged in conversation. The professor turned into the college road several hundred yards, and then stopped at one of the college buildings. Professor Holmes got out on the left side and started around the back of the car to go to the Old Chapel building on his right. The student got out of the right side and started around the back of the car to go to the Chemistry building on the left. The two of them met at the back of the car. Professor Holmes stopped suddenly, looked at the student, extended his hand and greeted him as a long lost friend. "Why, hello, my good friend, I haven't seen you in a long time. How have you been?"

THE ALERT-MINDED STUDENT

If in the minds of students, professors are to be classified as absent-minded, conversely students must classify themselves as ever present or alert-minded, which seems to be the case. Within the last year of my college teaching experience, I met up with a chap in one of my classes who is truly representative of this sort of student thinking. An Irish individual, alert in everything except his class assignments, in which he is often not prepared, gave a rather sharpwitted answer to a request I had made.

I had been lecturing one day in a duller than my usually dull fashion and I noticed a boy sitting next to the Irish chap who was comfortably sleeping and quite immune to the business of the classroom. So I addressed the Irish chap. "Jim,"

I said, "wake up your fellow student next to you." Jim's quick and surprising reply was, "You wake him up, professor; you put him to sleep."

A PROFESSOR WITH A SENSE OF HUMOR

The story is told of the professor's experience who had, on a certain class meeting, just prior to the Christmas holiday, elected to give an examination to his students. When the examination papers were turned in the professor learned that one member of the class had not answered the questions but instead had written, "Only God knows the answers to these questions," below which he had added, "Merry Xmas." The professor responded most definitely to what the student had written and acted accordingly.

Upon a subsequent meeting of the class when the professor had returned the papers, the student found not only a perfunctory failure indicated on the paper but an expression from the professor which showed he, too, had imagination. The professor had written, "God gets an A, you get an F, Happy New Year."

A STORY OF INTEREST TO COLLEGE AUDIENCES

Too many college teachers have become more concerned about the examination in their courses than about the student examined. Interest in testing, which gets to overshadow the interest in teaching, can too easily become a disease among college professors.

Mr. Burgess Johnson in his recent book *Campus Versus Classroom* relates this interesting story about examinations.

At least half a century ago Yale University passed through a period when the examining and marking enthusiasts ran amuck. In that day examinations were marked on a scale of two hundred, and some teachers became so enthusiastic that they went below zero and used the minus quantities.

There is a legend that one of these enthusiastic markers was approached after class by a student from the back row who said, "I wish you'd tell me, Professor, just how I stand now." The professor got out his record book: "I am sorry to have to tell you, Jones, that your standing is minus seventy-two." Jones tried to look properly downcast. "Gee, Prof," he said cheerfully, "I'll have to work like hell, won't I, to get up to zero?"

BISHOP SHEEN ON PROFESSORS

In the opening section of this book an anecdote is used revealing a dialogue between Nicholas Murray Butler, when he was president of Columbia University, and one of his eminent professors, Brander Matthews, regarding the difference between plagiarism and research in the use of the story.

Bishop Sheen's opinion may be added to what the two educators had to say.

Said the eminent divine, "If you copy anything out of one book, it is plagiarism. If you copy it out of two books, it is research. If you copy it out of six books, you are a professor."

THE CANDIDNESS OF PRESIDENT ELIOT

Dr. Lawrence Kimpton, the chancellor of the University of Chicago, is apparently a very humble and honest man. Soon after he was made chancellor he was asked to speak at the rather exclusive Executives' Club of Chicago, an assignment which he approached with some temerity. His remarks include a rather humorous anecdote.

He said, "I am honored and embarrassed in being asked

to speak to the Executives' Club, because I have reviewed the names of your past speakers, and I am flattered to be in such company. I'm very new at a very large job, and any storehouse of wisdom upon which I might draw my remarks is still to be built. I'm now at the stage of terrified innocence that Nicholas Murray Butler was many years ago when he had been president of Columbia for about six months. He was talking to President Eliot of Harvard who had been in office for some years, and he said to him, "This is a terrible kind of job we have. Have they ever called you a liar?"

"Called me a liar? Man," said Eliot, "they've proved it."

VOLUMES, VOLUMES EVERYWHERE

During a recent visit to a small Eastern college by an evaluation committee for one of the educational accrediting agencies, a tour of inspection of the campus buildings was being made. The committee had reached the library, the newest building on the campus; and for the most part were impressed with its furnishings and fine library equipment, and the books themselves.

In turn each member of the committee had remarked to the librarian about the fine library and its equipment. Excepting one.

He, looking intently and seeing few students, apparently was wondering whether the library was being put to full use, for he surprised the librarian by asking, somewhat facetiously, "Where is the other library?" Quite astonished the librarian replied, "The other library?"

"Yes," said the committee member, "the one the students use."

IN THE SAME VEIN

Not an evaluation committee, but a group of educators were visiting a school whose fine buildings and equipment gave the impression that it was blessed with funds and bene-factors.

The educators inspected new and well-equipped class-rooms and laboratories, a fine new field house and looked over the athletic fields with the dean. They were impressed.

"My!" exclaimed one of the group, "how many students do you have here?"

"Well, let me see," mused the dean, a wise member of the old school, and then thoughtfully and with seeming con-viction answered, "I'd say, about one in a hundred."

A CLASSROOM STORY

While this story does not have the college classroom for its source, in light of college students' difficulty with the use of the English language, it could very easily come from there.

A teacher in the grades had had particular trouble with a boy who had difficulty with his verbs, especially the irreg-ular verbs. He was unable to distinguish between, or use correctly, the past tense and the present perfect tense of these verbs. The one which bothered him most was the verb *go*. To the constant annoyance of the teacher he always said, "I have went," instead of, "I have gone." One day in class recitation when using the verb form in a sentence, to the teacher's com-plete disturbance, he said, "I have went home." The teacher told him to remain after school and write, one hundred times, "I have gone home."

After school, he sat down to his appointed task. When he had finished the teacher was not in the room so he put his paper on the desk and wrote her this note: "Dear Teacher, I have written, I have gone home one hundred times, and now *I have went home.*"

A PROFESSOR WITH THE HUMAN QUALITY

Too many college professors are afraid to relax. I know the importance of impressing students with the fact that a serious attitude toward courses is necessary for proper results in education. Too often, however, seriousness to the point where a teacher dispenses subject matter with the routine manner of a robot and students are viewed as automata is unfortunate for real education of personalities. There is too much formality in the college classroom today, and teachers' attitudes are too impersonal. This does not mean to let the bars down so that teaching effectiveness may be impaired. It does suggest, however, that the teacher must recognize the importance of the human element. The student is human, and the teacher shouldn't forget he also is supposed to be. Academic dignity, or pseudo-professional dignity, too often interferes with a human quality in teaching, or just plain naturalness on the part of the teacher.

Great teachers have this human quality. William Lyon Phelps of Yale was always cited as a teacher of warmth and understanding.

This little story concerns one of the two famous teachers —William and Henry James, teachers at Harvard. One of the famous teachers lectured occasionally at Radcliffe, the ladies' division of Harvard, and had in his class the contemporary writer, Gertrude Stein. Prof. James gave an examination one day to the class of which the eminent Gertrude was a member. Upon examining the papers, the professor was surprised to find Miss Stein's paper a complete blank, with the exception of a brief inscribed message reading: "Sorry, professor, I don't feel like writing an examination today."

As the story goes, Professor James returned the paper to Gertrude upon which he had written: "I know exactly how you feel, Gertrude, I often feel that way myself," and gave her an 'A'. Human, heh!

THE HUMAN TOUCH MAY SOMETIMES GO AWRY

We had been studying foreign expressions and idioms in one of my English classes and among them was the French idiom *savoir-faire.*

The term had brought to my mind a rather interesting story built around the term, so I engaged in a little levity and told the class this story.

An American professor met three staid members of the *Academie Francaise* in Paris and asked for their definition of *savoir-faire* which he wanted to include in his modern dictionary. "Eet is not deefeecult," one said. "Eef I go home and find my wife in the arms of another man and he is kissing her, I teep my hat to them and say: 'Excuse me.' That is *savoir-faire.*"

"No, that is not eet," said the second. "If I go home and find my wife in the arms of another man and he is kissing her, I teep my hat and say, 'Excuse me, continue,' that is *savoir-faire.*"

"No—not quite," rumbled the third, fingering his beard. "Eef I go home and find my wife in the arms of another man and kissing him, I teep my hat and say: 'Excuse me. Continue,' if he can continue—he has savoir faire."

At a later date, when I had asked the class to write on the meanings of the foreign expressions, one of the students had written for *savoir-faire* "that is when a professor goes home and finds his wife in the arms of another man."

Adapted From Irving Hoffman in
The Hollywood Reporter

AND WHO'S BLUSHING NOW?

Somewhere in this volume reference is made to Robert Lewis Taylor's recent biography of Winston Churchill, a highly popular publication. In fact, author Robert Taylor has authored six successful books.

Evidence reveals that as a student in a Southern Illinois University he occasionally had scholarship tangles with his professors in the field of English. Since English is literally his stock in trade, he must as he looks back, smile complacently as he thinks of the evaluation a teacher placed on one writing assignment she gave him.

Taylor has had no need to make reference to the teacher's feeling about his writing then, but being gracious about the affair, she has amusingly done it for him.

A recent Associated Press story under the Caption "Zany Student—Now Author" reports the occasion in interesting anecdote fashion.

Professor May T. Smith, Mr. Taylor's English teacher, says he was one of her poorest students. She recalls:

"Once when asked to write something he turned it into a wild conglomeration of impossible situations that had not the remotest connection with the assignment.

"His paper was returned fairly blushing with red ink, the recollection of which makes me do the blushing now.

"I've wished many times since that I had kept that zany

story. It would be worth a tidy sum now in the hands of his publishers."

Perhaps.

LLOYD DOUGLASS POSES A QUESTION FOR A PROFESSOR

The late Lloyd Douglass, the novelist, was visiting a friend of his at Pennsylvania State University, a professor of experimental psychology.

He came upon him one day in his laboratory intently watching the progress of a white rat run through a maze, inside a large box he had constructed. At each end of the box, terminating the maze, was a hole through which the rat would poke his nose as he came to either end. Douglass, after watching the professor with watch in hand observing the antics of the white rat, finally said, "And what is the purpose of all this?"

"Well," said the professor, "in running the maze, the rat went from one end to the other on the first trip in 20 seconds and stuck his nose out on completion. Returning, he made the trip to the other end showing his nose in 16 seconds. On the third trip he was able to return and show his nose in 12 seconds, so he would be making the return trip in approximately eight seconds."

Before the professor could continue, Douglass interrupted him and said, "Oh, I see, you are trying to determine how long it will take the rat so his nose is sticking out of both ends at the same time."

THE EXPERTS DON'T ALWAYS KNOW THE ANSWERS

Dr. Karl Becker, the one-time eminent Cornell professor, was examining a group of Ph.D. candidates with some other professors. Becker posed a seemingly profound question for one of the candidates, who squirmed, showing no signs of being able to answer it and calmly said that he didn't know the answer.

Several of the examining group seemed awed by the completeness with which Becker had stumped the candidate. As the group broke up, one of Becker's confreres went to him and said, "What is the answer to your question, Karl?"

Becker replied with complete casualness, "I don't know, the candidate should know. I'm *asking* the questions."

THE "PROFESSOR" STORY

Bennett Cerf, the well-known raconteur, tells a story of a Columbia University professor in his popular *"Try and Stop Me"* collection.

The late Irwin Edman, professor of philosophy at Columbia University, spent an evening with a colleague and his wife, and the conversation was spirited until about two o'clock in the morning. After several elaborate yawns had been ignored, the colleague said, "Irwin, I hate to put you out, but I have a nine o'clock class in the morning."

"Good Lord," said Irwin, blushing violently. "I thought you were at my house!"

"Great fleas have little fleas upon their backs to bite them, And little fleas have lesser fleas, and so ad infinitum . . . ."

And so with the stories of professors, they seem interminable. And here is one more. It seems to be the prototype for many stories of its kind; about many professors in as many institutions. It could have originated anywhere. But the professor's wife who told me the story, in her own unpretentious way, thinks it could have only happened to her husband.

In Greenville, Pennsylvania, is a small fine Lutheran institution, Thiel College. The head of one of the departments is Dr. Raymond Wagner, an amiable fellow and a good teacher.

Dr. Wagner had been asked to speak at Allegheny College, a neighboring institution twenty-five miles away at Meadville. The professor drove his car to Meadville, gave his speech, after which he walked down the street and had a bite to eat and in seemingly natural sequence went to the Erie Railroad station and got on the ten o'clock train for Greenville.

Upon arriving home his wife questioned him about how he got home. "I came on the train, of course," the professor said. And then she reminded him that he had driven his car to Meadville.

The next day Dr. Wagner went to the Erie depot, and conscious of having to make the trip from Greenville to Meadville and home again he purchased a round-trip railroad ticket to go and get his car in Meadville.

RATIO OF "THE BIG THREE" GRADUATES

A Boston brokerage house advertised for a "young Harvard graduate or the equivalent." Among the answers was one from a Yale man: "When you speak of an equivalent," he wrote, "do you mean two Princeton men or a Yale man half time?"

FROM YALE'S WILLIAM LYON PHELPS

Years ago the late William Lyon Phelps, one of Yale's most fabulous and finest professors, was approached for advice by a young newly-appointed teacher fresh out of graduate school. Phelps' counsel was as follows:

"Experience has taught me more than the theoretical study of pedagogy. You will doubtless find in your teaching that when you are holding forth there will be some lad in the class who will disagree with you. You will be tempted to nail him down and convert him right there and then. Don't do it. No doubt he is the only one who is listening."

A STUDENT'S APPRECIATION OF
THE SAME BILLY PHELPS

Dean Luther Weigle of Yale Divinity School tells this story about his son Dick and William Lyon Phelps, the Yale teacher.

Upon his son's graduation from Yale, Weigle asked him from what course in his college career did he think he got the most?

To his surprise, his son answered: "Billy's T & B" (He meant the course of Tennyson and Browning taught by Professor Phelps.)

He asked his son, "Why?"

To which Dick, after brief thought, replied, "I suppose because it gave me more to tie to and live by."

A STUDENT WHO DIDN'T APPRECIATE
ROBERT FROST

Some years ago I spent a delightful summer teaching at the Breadloaf School of English, conducted by Middlebury College. Two of my faculty associates giving courses that summer were the late Hervey *(Anthony Adverse)* Allen and Robert Frost, the poet, and I spent many pleasant hours walking the trails of the Green mountains and talking with these unusual men of American Literature. One soon learned they were both impatient with the usual classroom methods. They would readily hold class beside a mountain stream, under an apple tree, or on a trail. Formal examinations had little appeal for them. The deep and finer meanings of literature, and a desire to impart them to humans, were their only interests.

Recent years of teaching poetry appreciation to the boys at Amherst College hasn't changed Robert Frost's sense of values about teaching.

It is reported his method of teaching his course at Amherst is to give informal talks at his home in the evening. As is expected he detests formal examinations, but it is said he has reluctantly conformed to administrative policy, and gives them occasionally.

The poet says, "I have made them as simple as possible. Once I asked only one question, 'What good did my course do you?' and I requested brief replies. The answer I liked best was, 'Not a damn bit!' "

"Did you pass him?" Frost was asked.

"Yes, I gave him a 90."

"Why not 100?"

"He left the 'n' off damn."

SOMETIMES THEY AREN'T LISTENING

It could be there is a perfect answer to, "What's wrong with the movies and television?"

A student was asked to read aloud a paragraph from an essay which the instructor had chosen to help improve the students' comprehension of what they read. The student read the paragraph in a dull and labored manner. The instructor then asked him to restate the ideas or thought of the passage.

His earnest reply brought forth an hilarious response from the whole class. For he replied, "I am sorry, sir, but I wasn't listening."

OLD BUT GOOD

Here is an anecdote which has been going the rounds for several years but will always have appeal and rates inclusion here.

A chemistry professor asked his class what they considered the most outstanding contribution chemistry had made to the world.

Without hesitancy one student shouted out, "Blondes!"

WOODROW WILSON'S ANSWER

After years of teaching political science at Princeton University, Woodrow Wilson was finally elevated to the presidency of the institution, and he served faithfully until he entered political life.

He found as the chief administrative officer of the school that a problem which gave him concern was the constant inquiry of the parents, "Why Princeton wasn't doing more for their sons."

After trying for years to analyze and give a helpful and particular answer for each case, he finally came to the conclusion the reason was the same in practically every case, and his answer was always the same.

"Perhaps the reason we are not doing more for your son, is because he's your son."

WOODROW WILSON'S
RESULTING EDUCATION PHILOSOPHY

It is apparent that Woodrow Wilson's stock reply to parents of students who asked him while president of Princeton,

"Why isn't Princeton doing more for our son?" definitely influenced his philosophy concerning the purpose of a university in respect to boys' education.

In a speech, some time after he left Princeton, he said, "The use of a university is to make young gentlemen as unlike their fathers as possible."

NOT TO PLACATE PLAGIARISTS

Here is an interesting little anecdote for professors or teachers to use, which they can tell in a spirit of levity to students who are bent on borrowing or appropriating material, for their written assignments, from reputable sources.

The anecdote came from the notes of the late Dr. Frederick Welch, head of the English Department at the University of the North, which he had planned to use together with some other material in a proposed textbook for plagiarists.

The late professor told his students that if there were fraternity or sorority files from which they and their brothers or sisters were in the habit of borrowing manuscripts, they should not forget to give them current dates. For you wouldn't want to be caught like the lad in the classic story of beginning plagiarists who, when his paper was returned, found that the veteran professor had written on it: "I gave your father a C on this paper nineteen years ago and I still think it's not worth any more."

EDUCATION AND THE GIFTED CHILD

One of the constant criticisms directed at education is that it has failed to make provision for the child who is gifted and can do school work beyond the level of his student associates. Class regimentation retards his progress.

Here is a little story which may be used by discerning educators and laymen to illustrate the point:

One day a book salesman had come upon a teacher of the first or second years of the primary grades as she was taking her students at recess into the play yard.

As he talked with the teacher, two or three jet planes swiftly sped above them and disappeared. Two or three of the young boys immediately noticed them and talked about them in knowing phrases. "Boy," said one of them, "what speed; they can really penetrate the sound barrier." "Sound barrier nothing," responded another, "they can develop supersonic and hypersonic speeds, something the old reciprocal propeller jobs couldn't do."

They engaged in comment befitting aeronautical engineers as the salesman and the teacher both listened with delight.

Finally one of the little fellows said, "I wish they would come back." Another disgustedly replied, "Well, they won't, so we might as well go in and thread those damn heads."

Of course this indicates only too well that the school activities and endeavors, in which students are obliged to engage, are often a far cry from the interests and capabilities of many of them.

THE TRAVELING PROFESSOR

Professors who travel may often have trouble remembering their destination, how to get home and whether they came by car or train. In the case of one professor he had difficulty remembering where his berth was on the train. This somewhat facetious story illustrates the point.

The professor had left his berth in the sleeper to find a drink of water and was hopelessly lost in the middle of the car, unable to find his berth. It was midnight and the train was speeding through the country.

"Don't you remember the number of your berth?" asked the porter.

"I'm—ah—afraid not," was the reply.

"Well, haven't you some idea where it is?"

"Why, oh—yes, to be sure." The professor's face brightened.

"I did notice one time this afternoon that the window looked out upon a small lake."

FORMER GIRL STUDENT RETURNS

Student: "I wonder if you remember me? Years ago you asked me to marry you."

Absent-minded Professor: "Ah, yes, and did you?"

INSTRUCTOR WITH A SENSE OF HUMOR

In an attempt to have a little fun at the expense of the dean of women at the rather straight-laced Western Pennsylvania college where he taught, a young instructor told this story at a sorority banquet where the girls had their boy friends. The following letters reveal the story he told:

Letter Written by a Fraternity of a Neighboring College to the Dean

Dear Miss Phillips:

We have met some of the girls of your college and what we have seen we like very much. We would like to see more of them. We are having a dance here at the 'Phi Gam' house on the 19th, at which we would like to entertain some of the girls of your school. Would you write saying you will allow some of the girls to attend?

Respectfully yours,
John Williams
Fraternity Social Chairman

The Dean's Reply Read in Part

Dear Mr. Williams:

In reply to your note I shall be happy to allow some of our girls to attend your dance. In fact, I shall send a dozen of my best and most trustworthy girls.

Sincerely yours,
Ada Phillips
Dean of Women

The Social Chairman's Reply

Dear Miss Phillips:

Thank you for your note saying you would send a dozen of your best and most trustworthy girls to our dance.

Would it be possible to send half a dozen of that kind and a half dozen of the others?

Very cordially yours,
John Williams
Fraternity Social Chairman

PRESIDENT GIVES THE EDUCATOR HOPE

Charles W. Eliot, president of Harvard University for forty years and advocate of the humanities and father of the elective system of college courses, grew steadily younger in the eyes of the undergraduates. Shortly before his retirement, Eliot said: "When I was elected president, I was only thirty-five. Of course, I was very dignified, and I suppose a little frightening. As I walked about the campus, students would point at me and say: 'There goes old Eliot.'

"But now that I am seventy-five," he continued, "they look at me and say: 'There goes Charlie.'"

PROFESSOR STEPHEN LEACOCK'S ADVICE

During my teaching years at Middlebury College in Vermont, on my numerous trips to Montreal, which was not too far distant, I often visited McGill University where Stephen Leacock, one of Canada's most interesting authors, was a teacher of English.

Leacock's writings are pretty generally included in the college anthologies, particularly some of the humorous pieces from his "Literary Lapses."

Whenever he was asked by ambitious would-be authors to impart his magic formula for writing success, particularly along the humorous line, he would reply, "It is not hard to write funny stuff. All you have to do is to procure a pen and paper, and some ink, and then sit down and write it as it occurs to you."

"Yes, yes," the would-be writer would assent.

"The writing is not hard," Leacock would conclude, "but the occurring—that, my friend, is the difficulty."

STUDENT REPARTEE

Students at a small Pennsylvania college attest to the validity of this story. The wife of the college president had invited some of the campus leaders to a tea.

A number of the boys invited were served tea and were cluttered in one room. The president's wife in an effort to break up the congestion and get some of the boys in another room, approached a group of them and said, "There are some nice cookies in the other room, if you'd like them."

The boy nearest her surprised her by replying, "No, thanks, I've already got a date with a blonde in this room."

AN ABSENT-MINDED BIOLOGY PROFESSOR

I recently heard a student who is a biology department laboratory assistant tell this story about his biology professor, the absent-minded type, at a banquet meeting of a biology honor society.

"This afternoon Professor Swift announced the laboratory, today, would be devoted to the dissection and critical study of the leopard frog. Before starting his usual preliminary comments or lecture Professor Swift said, 'As we did not have a specimen of the leaping frog in the laboratory I have secured a very fine one,' at which point he reached into his pocket and drew out a paper bag which he emptied on the lab table. Out rolled a badly squashed ham sandwich.

" 'My goodness!' he stammered, mopping his brow, 'I distinctly remember eating my lunch.' "

PLAYWRIGHT BARRIE'S FAVORITE STORY

Sir James Barries's favorite story is reported to be about a professor of biology who explained to his class the spawning of fish. "So you see," he concluded, "the female fish deposits her eggs, the male fish comes along and fertilizes them, and later the little fish are hatched." One of the girls held up her hand. "You mean, Professor, that the father and mother fish—that they—that before that nothing happens?"

"Nothing," said the professor, "which doubtless explains the expression, 'Poor fish.' " ·

PROFESSOR'S WIFE TOLERANT

"Will is becoming the most absent-minded person I know," remarked a professor's wife to the wife of another professor.

"What's he been doing now?" inquired the friend.

"Why, this morning he thought he'd left his watch at home, and then took it out to see if he had time to go back and get it."

"That isn't as bad," said the friend speaking reminiscently of her equally absent-minded professor husband, "as the time when Frank left his office and put out a card saying he'd be back at 3:00 P.M. He started to leave and then finding he'd forgotten something, went back to his office, read the notice on the door and sat down on the stairs to wait until three o'clock until he returned."

CHAPTER SEVEN

Stories from the
Field of Sports

Sport that wrinkled Care derides,
And Laughter holding both his sides
—Milton

It seems there is no better occasion for the fine spirit engendered by a good story than a sports gathering or banquet, and the most appropriate and the most appreciated story is from the field of sport itself. Such noted raconteurs as Fritz Crisler, the former Michigan coach and still director of athletics at Michigan, and Jimmy Conzelman, another famous football mentor, have enhanced their reputations by being adept speakers and storytellers on the banquet circuit. Perhaps the greatest storyteller among the sports coterie was the late Knute Rockne. The overtones of this great spirit have never died nor his stories which are still told at sports get-togethers. One of Knute's players and later coach at Notre Dame, Frank Leahy, established quite a reputation for himself as a speaker. Frank learned early the value of public speaking and set about to train himself. He has always been in demand.

These outstanding figures of the world of sport have not confined their storytelling to the sports field, but have been equally adept in telling other stories, usually humorous stories.

SPORT STORIES HAVE BROAD USE AND APPEAL

Because of the universal appeal for and interest in sports there is a corresponding common interest in stories about sports, and about the figures and personalties associated with them.

The sports story, however, goes beyond any intrinsic value it may have in relation to sport itself and, therefore, should find popular use with all speakers. It is a wise speaker who will recognize the broad application of many sports stories and adopt their use.

Some time ago Representative Torbert MacDonald of Massachusetts introduced a bill to enlarge our cultural exchange program to include sports, which apparently has been put into action, because some of our outstanding athletes are already carrying on goodwill assignments abroad.

Representative MacDonald is a good man to have introduced such a measure because he was a star halfback at Harvard and an exceptional track man. He played baseball for the New York Yankees for awhile, and if he had been willing to wait out the tenure of some of the Yankee stars, he no doubt would have stayed with the ball club.

When asked about the progress of the sports bill he indicated, that considering the limited amount of work he did, the interest of his constituents was amazing.

He further added, ". . . the amount of praise you get in this job has no relation to the amount of work you do. All I did was drop this sports bill of mine into the hopper and I began receiving all kinds of praise and congratulations from my constituents . . . But I have been knocking myself out for weeks fighting the natural gas lobby, and not one of my constituents is even aware of it."

And this about expresses it. There is a strong and intense interest in the American sport scene and in every phase of its activity.

The stories included in this section are devoted to or derived from the various fields of sport. For the most part they contain a good element of humor, and where this is not the case their value is high in human interest and philosophy. The stories of the latter type have special adaptability for speeches of all kinds where stories are used,

THE FANS NEVER MISS A CHANCE

Joe Williams, the sports columnist, has been credited with this story, but it has been suggested he may have gotten it from Jimmy Conzelman, a former outstanding coach, in slightly different form. It, however, has value for those who speak at sport gatherings.

At a Northwestern football game the alumni, seated in the stands behind the Northwestern bench, were exhorting their heroes. Suddenly the situation changed. Northwestern fumbled three times and each fumble led to a touchdown for the other side. Finally Lynn Waldorf, the Northwestern coach at that time and now coach of the University of California "Golden Bears," motioned to two of his reserve backs.

"I'm sending you fellows in and I want you to be sure to hold on to the ball. These fumbles are making us look ridiculous. And just to be sure take a ball and warm up on the sidelines first."

This the two reserve backs proceeded to do. They indulged in a brisk game of pitch and catch with the football and in turns served as center to pass to the other. Just before the warm-up was ended one of the backs fumbled and the ball bounded away about ten yards. Seeing this, one of the old grads staggered to his feet and yelled: "All right, coach, put him in. He's ready."

RED SMITH TELLS A "QUICKIE"

Writing about the Princeton-Harvard game of November, 1948, in which Princeton maltreated Harvard by piling up 47 points to Harvard's 7, New York's Sportswriter 'Red' Smith makes a sly observation which suggests the possibility that some college football teams have gone "big time." (Considering the present policy of operation adopted by the Ivy League, where spring practice has been abolished and where there is no semblance of recruiting athletes, the idea of the story may not apply to the present situation, although it may have in the past and applies to other schools now.)

After discussing the relative play of the two teams, Smith concludes: "It was especially clear that this Princeton-Harvard game was, above all else, a Big Three game. A man selling programs outside the stadium had left no doubt of that. 'Get your program,' he shouted. 'The names, numbers and salaries of all the players.' "

THE ROSE BOWL PASSED THEM UP

Andy Kerr, famous football coach of yesteryear, coached a 1932 Colgate team that won all its games and wasn't scored upon. When this remarkable aggregation was not invited to play at the Pasadena Rose Bowl, as had been expected, Mr. Kerr gave voice to the immortal remark: "Undefeated, unscored upon, untied and uninvited."

THE LATE "BO" McMILLIN TOLD THIS ONE ON HIMSELF

Centre College, Kentucky, in 1955, had its first undefeated season since the days of its greatest halfback, Alvin "Bo" McMillin. In the early twenties he led a great team to an undefeated season which featured a win over a rugged Harvard team. A few years ago the sports pages carried a news story which told of the death of the great McMillin. "Bo" was truly mourned by untold numbers of those interested in sports and by the coaching profession generally. He had established a unique niche for himself as a football player, and by his character and keen sense of football values he had made a solid contribution to the coaches' organizations. They, as well as the fans, will miss the beloved "Bo."

The late McMillin, former Indiana University and Detroit Lions Coach, and more recently coach of the Philadelphia Eagles professional football team, used to tell a story about a time when he was playing for the "Praying Colonels" of Centre College and was in the doghouse with Coach Charley Moran. As a result, Moran kept the popular "Bo" on the bench while the fans in the stands kept yelling, "We want McMillin!"

This went on for some time until finally Moran ceased ignoring "Bo" and beckoned to him. Off came McMillin's top jacket and he began to limber up on the sideline.

"Who do I go in for, Coach?" he asked.

"You don't go in for anybody," said Uncle Charley. "Just go up in the stands with your friends. They want you more than I do."

FROM THE FAMOUS FOOTBALL COACH, POP WARNER

"Pop" has successfully told this story, but it is definitely in the class of the "pun" and the pun sometimes, unless deftly told, has a habit of recoiling. It is still a good one.

In the early days of his career, "Pop" Warner coached at the Carlisle Indian School where he turned out great teams which were matched with Harvard, Army and other leading college elevens in the country. He produced, among others, such famous stars as the great Jim Thorpe, Guyon, and Calac.

He relates that on one of his teams he had a splendid halfback, but he had one great fault. Every time a play was called when this back was to carry the ball, he always showed it because his face flushed all over, and the opposing players soon realizing this were able to stop him before he got started. "Pop" said he tried everything to break the Indian of the habit, but he had no success. Finally, he realized there was only one solution to it and he acted on it. He got three other halfbacks who flushed, too, and as a result he had a perfect backfield of four-flushers.

JIM THORPE TELLS ONE

Fred Benham, a New York publicist, was talking one time to the great Thorpe and he asked Jim if there were any material about him that hadn't been done to death in the papers.

"Yes . . . one thing," grunted Thorpe. "I'm a twin. My twin brother died when we were five . . . or six."

"How did it happen?" asked Fred Benham.

"We were raised on canned milk," replied Jim seriously, "and we ran out of cans."

SPEAKING OF COACHES

Ohio State University's search for a new head football coach to succeed Wes Fesler was on in earnest a few years ago.

President Howard L. Bevis told a capacity audience at the annual football appreciation dinner at the time:

"We'll look over the entire field, in and out of the university, and we'll hire the best man we can find. We'll try to find a genius—a man who never makes the same mistake once."

Well, the committee who found the new coach, apparently did just that. For in the person of Woody Hayes the Buckeyes seem to have a genius. It has not taken him long to sat-

isfy Ohio State alumni and fans. He has won the Big Ten
Championship the last two years, but what is more, the Buckeyes, in so doing, have accomplished their greatest and
seemingly impossible goal. They have put an end to the
defeat regime administered to them by Michigan. And in
running over the Wolverines last year they made it possible
for Michigan State, the Conference runner-up, who lost to
Michigan, to be the Big Ten Rose Bowl representative. Ohio
State was the Rose Bowl contender last year, but the conference ruling will not allow representation by the same team
two years in a row. So Michigan State backed in as the contender.

LEAHY'S MOTTO: "MAKE THE PUNISHMENT
FIT THE CRIME"

Admirers of Notre Dame's Frank Leahy placed him in
a class with the great Knute Rockne. Whether he was or not,
the fact remains he had one trait in common with Rockne,
the ability to have a ready answer or make a quick retort.

This story about him is culled from the chapter written
about the outstanding coach in Edwin Pope's fine book
"Football's Greatest Coaches" which reveals the full overtones of Frank Leahy's personality.

"If Leahy did not always have the right answer, at least
he always had an answer. When his Boston College team
left by train for New Orleans and a game with Tulane, he
moaned, "Here we are idling about on the train, getting stiff
while that big Tulane bunch is working out and improving."
A few weeks later, just before the University of Idaho squad
entrained for Boston to play Boston College, an assistant told
Leahy not to worry—the vandals were a pushover. "What!"
Leahy snapped. "Not worry about them! How can I help

worrying, with them resting up on a leisurely train ride east while we wear ourselves out at practice."

Such an anecdote as this has a place in a sport talk which deals with the almost common peculiarity of coaches who constantly refuse to take an encouraging outlook in respect to approaching games.

ANOTHER STORY ABOUT
MICHIGAN'S "FRITZ" CRISLER

H. O. "Fritz" Crisler, director of athletics at the University of Michigan, called "The Most Self-possessed Man" includes among his accomplishments a reasonable wit which he often puts to advantage speaking before clubs in the Detroit area, and often at meetings generally across the country.

By some who have known him it is not felt his sense of humor came when he achieved fame as a coach, but was cultivated from the time he was a student.

One who knew Crisler's background was a gentleman named Thurston Davies who recently served as president of a Colorado college. Some years ago, I knew Davies well when he was headmaster of the Nichols School in Buffalo, where we often played informal basketball together. He left Buffalo in the early thirties to go to Princeton as a graduate manager of athletics to raise the Tiger's football stock which had reached an all-time low under Al Wittmer. The top item on Davies' agenda was to lure Crisler away from Minnesota to become coach at Princeton. Davies was impressed by Crisler as a coach, knowing full well there was no room for levity in his coaching philosophy.

In his public relations program the former University of Chicago end made full use of his native wit and humor in which Davies was interested to help unite a disturbed Princeton alumni and student body.

In his last year, 1931, at Minnesota Crisler had, in five months, made 103 speeches to Minnesota fans and alumni groups and cemented relations with the press, which had been seriously estranged. When he joined Princeton he literally raced around the country and spoke to every Princeton club which numbered close to a hundred. Princeton's stock rose. When he left the New Jersey school after the 1937 season his record was 25-9-5.

Princeton grads remember Crisler as coach. Many previously remembered him as a player opposing them. It was with him as a player that the following story is concerned, which was revealed to graduate manager Davies when Crisler went to the Princeton campus as coach.

"Back in his college days, Fritz was playing end for the University of Chicago in a game against Princeton. It was his job to handle Stanley Keck, the Tigers' All-American tackle. This he was doing in a highly capable manner which must have delighted his coach, the immortal Alonzo Stagg, for whom he later coached. In fact, Fritz was giving Keck a very bad afternoon and the Princeton star was getting more annoyed by the minute. Finally Fritz, a sharp student, through continued repartee, made the day a complete failure for Keck by saying: 'Listen, Mister, I don't know what your name is or what you are doing in the Princeton line-up. But unless you brace up and stop some of our plays pretty soon you can bet your coach will have that guy Keck in here. The papers say he's real good.' "

A UNIVERSITY PRESIDENT WITH
A SENSE OF HUMOR

Someone recently observed that professional football lost a colorful figure when Charlie (Choo Choo) Justice, a remarkable halfback a few years ago at the University of North Carolina, rejected flattering offers from the "pros." He finally catapulted and signed with the Washington Redskins.

It is said the little tarheel in his fantastic football career had almost as big a following as Red Grange. In some respects his popularity was even keener. Songs were published about him, and a campaign once was started to appoint him president of the University. Grange was deluged with praise, but the highest office anyone suggested for him was a directorship on the University of Illinois Board of Control.

During the Justice boom for president, "Bill" Carmichaels was acting president at the North Carolina school, and he entertained the proposal with quite a sense of humor. He needed one when a faction clamored for "Choo Choo" to be given Bill's job. His interesting reply to the proposal was:

> "I don't think anyone ought to support Justice for the job of running the faculty. It would not be fair to ask Choo Choo and his family to live on the president's salary."

There were many reports that Tarheel alumni were paying the little halfback $15,000 a year to attend school and play football. Carmichaels had an answer for this:

"The $15,000 figure is untrue. "Choo Choo" is not getting a dime more than $13,500."

ANOTHER STORY ABOUT JUSTICE

"Ted" Hazelwood, a giant tackle and a team mate of Choo Choo Justice, had a keen respect for Choo Choo's habit of continually reversing his field when galloping for a touchdown. For instance, he might reach the thirty-yard line, and close to the outside of the opponents' territory, and finding himself blocked, would neatly turn back and race to the forty or fifty-yard line with his own interference and opponents chasing after him. He would then suddenly reverse his field again and start for the goal line, which he usually made. This practice he would repeat several times an afternoon in the course of a ball game.

Against Duke University, one afternoon, Hazelwood, our tackle, pinned an opposing player with a ferocious block and then sat on him. The victim finally screamed.

"Lemme up, ya big ape; Justice passed here ten seconds ago."

Continuing to sit on his opponent, Ted calmly refused saying: "Nothin' doing, buddy, Choo Choo may be back this way two or three times more before this play is over."

BILL McGEEHAN ON BOBBY JONES

During the period of the First World War and for some years after W. O. "Bill" McGeehan, the New York Tribune sports writer, was considered the dean of the sports writer's profession. Bill's writing was considered to be the acme of sports journalism, and his style was the standard which the young writers set for themselves. The secret of McGeehan's success lay in his ability to go beyond mere reporting of sports events; he was quick to observe the traits in great sports personalities which made them champions. McGeehan particularly admired Bobby Jones, the golfer, and no one was better able to reveal the spark behind the genius of this great competitor as he does in this little observation.

Back in the "twenties" Gene Sarazen and Bobby Jones were the finalists in the National Open Golf Tournament. After intense competition the master Jones won out. McGee-han head-lined his story of the event with the announcement: "Jones Wins National Open by Defeating Sarazen." In the story which followed the answer to Jones' greatness was suc-cinctly revealed. It ran: . . . "the defeat of Gene Sarazen, a fine golfer, in the National Open by the great competitor and master Bobby Jones is not difficult to understand. After watching these two great performers in a great match the reason is obvious: Sarazen played Jones; Jones played golf."

A STORY WHICH HAS MANY USES

The point of this story about two great competitors has unusual value in many speech situations. The great moral lesson to be derived from the fine competitive spirit of a Bobby Jones goes far beyond the game he represented and into the important values of life.

Such a story has a place not only in the speech which deals with sports, but in inspirational talks and sermons. Any-one who speaks to groups about how to play the game of life has a need for such stories.

The question is often raised, who was the greater golfer, Walter Hagen or Bobby Jones. Jones in 1930 won the four great championships, both the amateur and open crowns in both Britain and the United States, which immortalized him. In all he won thirteen top titles to Hagen's eleven. But on one occasion when the two met in match play, Hagen handed Bobby Jones his worst defeat.

Gene Sarazen, a great golfer himself, who played against both men corroborates the story above about Jones when he names Jones the world's no. 1 scorer and Hagen the no. 1 match player. "Jones," he says, "was at his best when he concentrated on licking par; Hagen when he could play his opponent."

Ted Shane, sportswriter, supports the idea that Hagen's greatness lay in playing his opponents; and the dramatic manner in which he played them. His sportsmanship, however, was unassailable, Shane says, but he was not beyond using guile in influencing his competitor.

There are numerous examples of this so-called guile employed by the colorful Hagen. This little anecdote illustrates it pretty well, as told by sportswriter Shane:

In one Professional Golfer's Association battle when Hagen's ball lay fifteen feet from the cup and his opponent's only seven, Walter looked up with a broad grin. "What's the joke?" his rival asked.

"I was just thinking how much harder your putt will look after I've made mine!" He sank his—the opponent missed by six inches.

DIZZY DEAN STILL AN AMERICAN INSTITUTION

Dizzy Dean played ball with the famous St. Louis Cardinals team of the gashouse gang which included such players as Frankie Frisch, Pepper Martin, "Ducky" Medwick and Dizzy's famous brother, Daffy. This is a far cry from the day of the present fan.

Since his playing days, Dizzy has become famous for his baseball broadcasts over a Cincinnati Station. His unorthodox diction has really made him an institution. More recently Dizzy shifted the scene of his activities to a New York television station where he was the commentator of the games televised by the New York Yankees. Last season he had the "Game of the Week" program on television.

Only recently a major league team baseball manager remarked that ball players today fail to show enough color in their playing and diamond activity. What they need, he said, is more of the spirit and color of Dizzy Dean.

What he failed to recognize is that they are not "Dizzy Deans" to begin with. Dean was a colorful personality, beyond his playing ability, because of what he was in the first place—Dizzy Dean.

MAE WEST KNEW HIM

Mae West, an equally important character in her chosen field, sometimes unduly prominent, had, it is reported, made a visit to the Pope. When her audience with him had finished, she remarked upon leaving in almost characteristic fashion, "Come up and see me sometime."

The Pope said he didn't think he could arrange it, but he would be happy to send up one of the Cardinals.

"Oh, one of the Cardinals, eh?" remarked Mae. "Well, send up Dizzy Dean."

A SPEAKER WISHES TO GET TO FIRST BASE AT LEAST

A Pittsburgh sports writer contributes this anecdote about the late Franklin D. Roosevelt. It seems to be especially appropriate for the speaker who may feel somewhat disoriented as he gets to his feet at an important gathering to begin his speech. He may, however, have to remove the stigma of the political party reference in the story. But it has great value for political speakers at election time.

On a summer night in 1932, Franklin Roosevelt and his campaign party moved into Forbes Field, the home of the Pittsburgh Pirates, for a big rally. F.D.R. was a rookie in the packed park and he displayed nervousness when he arose to speak on a platfrom erected near second base.

Flashes from one hundred cameras bewildered the Presidential nominee before he could begin his speech. Recovering from the shock, he said:

"My friends, I am confused by all this shooting. I scarcely know where I am standing."

He paused a moment, then added:

"Somebody near me just informed me that I am in the vicinity of second base—but what I would like to say is that I am chiefly concerned about getting to first base."

He reached first base in 1932, landed at second in '36, worked his way to third in '40 and scored an historic run in '44.

AN UMPIRE WHO COULDN'T SEE

Last spring I attended a bowling banquet as a guest. Another guest was Bill McKinley, the baseball umpire in the American Major League who makes his home in Kinsman, Ohio. Before the main speaker was introduced McKinley was called on for a few remarks. Bill responded by telling this story:

"There was a young umpire who was working games in the south during the training camp season of the ball clubs. The beginner was working under the wily and experienced eye of the veteran umpire, Bill McGowan. They had been working games together. One afternoon, during pre-game practice, it began to rain quite hard. Expecting it would continue, a few of the fans made for a nearby hotel and the

young umpire did likewise. He made for the grill and proceeded to get himself pleasantly drunk, or wet inside, as the
rain continued for about an hour outside. When it stopped,
the chief umpire, McGowan, decided to play the game, when
he suddenly missed the young arbiter. He had a suspicion
where he might be and hurried off to the hotel grill and
found him in a condition not fit for umpiring. As he was
badly needed, McGowan instructed him to take a cold shower
and report.

Very shortly after the young fellow made his way to
the ballpark, but still showing the effects. He took his place
at first base to umpire the base decisions, and the game
got under way. On the first play a ball was hit to the infield
and the throw caused a close play at first base, arriving about
the same time as the runner. The young umpire looked at
the play in a blurry-eyed manner, without calling the runner
out or safe. The opposing team's coach and the first baseman
descended on the bewildered umpire and yelled, "What is
he?" "What is he?," said the umpire, still confused, "What
is he? Where is he?"

A STORY FROM THE "YANKEE CLIPPER," JOE DiMAGGIO

Several years ago I was in charge of activities at the Lake
Champlain Club in Vermont. Among the guests with whom I
had the pleasure of spending considerable time was Joe
DiMaggio. I carry a photo taken with him as a memento of
the happy days together.

I was able, on the occasion of one of our enjoyable chats,
to draw a favorite story from him. The story is about Leo
Durocher, the former New York Giants Manager, who has
forsaken baseball for the more luminous field of entertain-

ment in Hollywood. It appears Joe had picked up the story from Bennett Cerf or someone else.

This is the story in substance as the great outfielder told it to me. Durocher, it appears, had the reputation for being the most accomplished needler in modern baseball. It was at the time, a few seasons back, when the Giants were playing their traditional pre-season game at West Point.

The Cadet Corps began to ride Leo as he passed up and down the coaching box at third base. "Hey, Durocher," roared one leather-lunged upper classman, "How did a runt like you ever sneak into the big leagues?"

"Leo," DiMaggio said, "silenced the uproar with a single retort. He just hollered back, 'My congressman appointed me.' "

GIANTS STILL PLAYING THE CADETS

The traditional game between the National Leaguers, now the San Francisco Giants, and West Point is still being played. Willie Mays and company, this spring, gave the Cadets a lesson in baseball. The following appeared under an A.P. dateline of May 27, 1958: "West Point, N.Y. The Giants smothered Army, 17-1, Monday in their annual game with the Cadets."

THE MAGIC OF A YANKEE UNIFORM

Some years ago, when I launched my teaching career at Middlebury College, the Vermont school had just previously enrolled and lost a student who was impatient with the scholastic life and decided to devote his interest to baseball. He developed into a prominent major-leaguer. He was Waite Hoyt, the former Yankee pitching great, to whom this story is credited. Waite has been given credit for the remark which started the rumor that a Yankee uniform works magic upon its wearer. "It's great to be young and be a Yankee," he once said.

Charlie Dexter, the sports writer, relates that Hoyt in his declining years as a pitcher was traded to the Pirates. It was the season of 1933, after the Bronx bombers had crushed the Cubs in four straight series games. Waite was on the mound for the Pirates against the Cubs. He wasn't at his best and the Bruin bench jockies were riding him unmercifully.

Hoyt called time, strode off the mound and faced the Cub dugout, "If you guys don't shut up," he snapped, "I'll put on my Yankee uniform and scare you to death!"

They shut up.

AND SO SAYS JOE DiMAGGIO

If Waite Hoyt supposedly started the rumor that there is magic in a Yankee uniform there were a few others who continued the important psychology. Joe DiMaggio points this out in that superb little book of his, *Lucky To Be A Yankee*. He credits its continuance and, perhaps, realization to that splendid character and peerless leader of the Yankees during their championship years of the thirties, Joe McCarthy. DiMaggio writes with conviction:

> *McCarthy acts on the theory that the only good ball players in the whole country are wearing Yankee uniforms and that once you put on a Yankee uniform you automatically become a better ball player. Maybe this sounds like kid stuff . . . , but all I know is that it works. It worked with me and it worked with others.*

THE MUCH BELOVED SPORT'S OFFICIAL

Like the baseball umpire who is accused of blindness when he makes decisions which displease the fans, this story suggests that most sports officials can't see at all.

A star of a winning high school basketball team was a young man whose sight was considerably impaired by a cataract in one eye. On the occasion of a certain game he had humbled his team's rivals by scoring basket after basket and emerged as high scorer and the stand-out player of the game.

Aside from receiving the plaudits of the fans and players, he also received the favor of the referee. Congratulating him after the game, the referee remarked, ". . . and I understand you are handicapped by a cataract in your eye." The player said it was true. The referee replied, "Well, it's unfortunate, but it's a good thing you have that one good eye." To which the player slowly, but intently replied, "Well, when I lose that, I'm going to become an official."

Some Sport Thoughts for Serious Speeches

THE REAL VALUE OF SPORTS

We hear it repeated so often it is a commonplace that the great values young men derive from participation in sports come not from the game itself but from the by-products which may be realized. All the great teachers and coaches in both the amateur and professional fields of athletics not only solidly subscribe to this, but religiously attempt to have it realized.

Coach Earl Blaik of the Army was not particularly disturbed because his team suffered three defeats last season, but he was able to attest to the satisfaction resulting from severe and testing adjustments made by the boys which made their victories possible. Blaik has often said that the football activity at the "Point" is not concerned primarily with making football players, but with developing officers. As a medium for accomplishing this, he feels football has no parallel.

He realizes the ultimate values it has in developing manhood. In respect to last year's squad he feels adjustments were necessary because of lack of player depth and the cribbing incident of 1951, which all but wiped out the squad. Referring to the situation Blaik says:

"I think the boys get more out of it, in the sense that there are a lot of sacrifices made. It's an uphill battle and it's the uphill battles that always bring out the best in men."

HALAS THOUGHT BEYOND FOOTBALL

George Halas, coach of the Chicago Bears professional football team, is another outstanding coach who has always been concerned about the values beyond the game itself.

A recent article commenting on Halas in respect to his influence on young men says:

"It's always been his idea that we are in something more than just football. He's always wanted his players to use the "pro" game as a stepping stone to more permanent things."

COACH KERR'S, "THIS I BELIEVE"

And listen to the great Andy Kerr, coach at Stanford University and Colgate among other schools, famous for his rueful remark, "Undefeated, unscored on—and uninvited!" after his 1932 Colgate team had established a (9-0-0) record and was then bypassed by the Rose Bowl in favor of the Pitt Panthers (who were slaughtered, 35-0, by Southern California). In an expression of his philosophy, delivered on Columbia Broadcasting System's "This I Believe," Kerr said:

"At the center of my philosophy of life has been the ideal of service; the desire to help my fellow man . . . .

"I believe in God, the Creator and Ruler of the universe. I hold that a man's religious faith is the greatest single force in his life for good . . . .

"My philosophy of life is based on faith in America and its institutions, in the youth of America . . . and in my work. I have faith in my family . . . and a necessary faith in myself. I have an abiding faith in God. In my life I have tried to express those faiths in service to my church, my community, and to mankind generally.

"This has given me a happy and satisfying philosophy of life."

Actuated by such thoughts Andy Kerr was a marked influence, through the years, upon the boys to whom he taught football. He had a great sense of the by-products of the game, and he was thereby able to impart real values for life.

It has been observed that few men achieve the rapport with young men or pupils Kerr did, and he was beloved by every player he coached. Edwin Pope in his "Football's Greatest Coaches" relates:

"One of his players at Washington and Jefferson, Dr. Delbert Secrist, says, 'My father died when I was a baby and my mother passed on when I was starting college. If it hadn't been for Andy, I don't know what I'd have done. He was like a father and mother rolled into one. He even taught us at Sunday School.' "

Pages could be written about the influence Andy Kerr had upon young men in helping them to mold better lives.

COACH FRANK LEAHY'S DIRECT MANNER

As pointed out elsewhere in this chapter Frank Leahy may have had much in common with his coach and one of his predecessors at Notre Dame, the late Knute Rockne. It is certain he profited much from experience and association with the great Rockne, and it is likely he learned the subtle and sometimes harsh and sarcastic method of dealing with players who let success go to their heads, what coaches often call cephalic inflation.

But Leahy, tradition has it, had a positive manner and directness in dealing with people and coveted it as a character trait and expected it from or tried to inculcate it into others. On one occasion he reprimanded a player with:

"You were in the open field and you fell! Did you trip over a chalk line? Or was it a newspaper clipping? And look me in the eye when I speak to you!"

FROM THE MASTER ROCKNE

It is said that nobody was quicker on the draw than Knute Rockne. Nobody had a better sense of the right touch to bring out the best in his players. He was never really abusive; never bullied but got results with sarcasm. If a player got out of line and felt as an individual he was more important than the team, or developed an unhealthy ego to the point where he was unable to take direction from the coach, Rockne worked him over. He used every opportunity to straighten him out, even though the punishment didn't always fit the crime.

CROWLEY OF THE FOUR HORSEMEN A SUBJECT

The famous four horsemen backfield at Notre Dame had a good day in a game with Princeton, but on one play Jim

Crowley was slow getting started and was overtaken from behind just as he was getting under way for one of his spectacular runs. Slagle, who became an All-American, was the tackler who brought him down.

Between the halves Crowley, who had been in the dog-house with Rockne, apologized for his mistake explaining he misjudged Slagle's speed and he should have cut back and eluded him.

"But that wasn't your mistake," answered Rockne.

"Yes, it was," insisted Crowley. "That was my mistake, and I want to admit it."

"No, that wasn't your real mistake," came back the famous coach. "Slagle didn't know who you were," and he continued, "You should have shown him some of your New York press clippings. If Slagle could have read how good you were, he wouldn't have dared come even close to you. That was your mistake."

To players who, just once, neglected to study their assignments, because there never was a second time, and messed up the execution of plays, Rockne employed a stock expression. "There are some dumb people and some dumber people," he would say and then add, "You come next."

And speaking of "I.Q's" it is claimed another favorite expression he often made to his guards and tackles was, "The only qualifications for a lineman are to be big and dumb." And not neglecting his backs, he added, "To be a back, you only have to be dumb."

A COACH WHO IMPARTED SPIRITUAL VALUES

Again Edwin Pope reflects the spirit of another great coach in respect to his influence upon the lives of young men.

Speaking of the great Nebraska University and Texas coach, Dana X. Bible, Pope says:

"Dana Xenophon Bible left a spiritual deposit slip in the heart of every boy he coached."

ON THE OTHER END OF THE SCALE

With the present emphasis on the importance of winning football games in college competition, a coach cannot talk about the great life values young men derive from the game to offset the stigma of continual losses.

The coach at Creighton college, Marchmont Schwartz, fans will remember as a former outstanding Notre Dame halfback, had a tough season a few years ago and his team lost a number of games.

After the season was over, Schwartz appeared as the main speaker at a banquet and was introduced not only as a coach who knew his football but as a builder of character.

In response, Marchie stated, "When your team wins every game, you're hailed as a great coach. But when your team drops three or four games you make them believe that the main purpose of football is to build character."

Still Sports—A Different Kind

BIG STAKES FOR BIG MEN

Herbert Bayard Swope, Bernard Baruch and a third gentleman were playing a high stakes poker game on a train . . . As benefited their positions they refused to play with anyone who wasn't an entertaining player as well as a good loser . . . A certain cinema producer had long aspired to get into a game with them . . . He was readily admitted . . . "Just a moment," he bragged, "none of this piker stuff for me. When

I play poker, I play high. Give me $10,000 worth of chips."
... To which Baruch turned to Swope and indifferently said:
"Okay, Herb—throw him a blue one."

THE SPORT OF COLORED WAITERS

The late Colonel E. R. Bradley of Palm Beach was invariably at the Saratoga races in August . . . He dwelt at the United States Hotel, where for fifteen years the same old colored waiter served him in the dining room. . . . One morning Bradley was confronted by a new waiter. . . . "Where's old Joe?" he asked. . . . "He's stationed at the other end," was the answer. . . . "Well, get him!" said Bradley. Old Joe appeared.

"Why aren't you waiting on me?" Bradley asked Joe.

"Sorry, Colonel," Joe explained, "But I lost you in a crap game."

ABOUT THE BALLPLAYER 'CAP' ANSON

The late Eddie Durling said he heard of a young fellow with a first name of Omaha. The name was inspired by his having been born in Omaha, Nebraska.

This brings to mind the tale told of the great Chicago ballplayer, "Cap" Anson, whose full name was Adrian Constantine Anson. When six he asked his mother why he had such "funny" names as Adrian and Constantine while the other kids were named John, George, Charles and Robert. His mother told him she was born in Adrian, Michigan, and his father in Constantine, Mich., so they named him Adrian Constantine. That night when little Adrian Constantine knelt in prayer, he thanked the Lord his mother had not been born in Ypsilanti and his father in Kalamazoo.

CHAPTER EIGHT

About Clergymen, the Church
and the Denominations

"There is no such thing as a really old joke. If you never heard it before, it's new."

—Bennett Cerf

Perhaps one of the most successful story categories is the one which provides opportunity, in a good wholesome way, to poke fun at the various church denominations and also the clergy; and certainly with no design to show disrespect or give any suggestion of the sacrilegious. The following stories in this class have always had high entertainment value, and come highly recommended by their users.

Every story in the group was told to me by speakers who used them, or I actually heard them used on a speaking occasion by some prominent person.

Some of the stories included here are not as old as the chestnut variety and yet are not the most modern. Some of them are older than those of you who shall read them, but they are stories which have lived and will live and are, therefore, in part, classics and bear retelling. As has been remarked, a gentleman has never heard a story before or as Bennett Cerf has observed, "good jokes, like good wines, mellow with age, . . . as so many wits have so truthfully insisted."

This is not an apology for re-using known stories, but Mr. Cerf further remarks, "Most so-called new stories are simply dressed up versions of chestnuts anyhow." So good stories among this group are of both the new and old variety.

AN EDUCATOR TELLS ONE ON THE METHODISTS

Dr. J. A. Brumbaugh, former vice-president of the American Council of Education in Washington, relates an interesting story told by a good friend of his, a Presbyterian clergyman, with a sense of humor.

The Presbyterian clergyman in question occupied his pulpit on Sunday and told his congregation that he was becoming tired of the Methodists in town who, in their complacency, were constantly directing barbs at the members of his church and at him, personally, for their so-called liberality, which the Methodist brethren were certain would lead the Presbyterians to no good end.

He said as a result he had arrived at the conclusion, which he had recently and quite emphatically made known to the Methodists, that he had decided he would rather be a so-called poor liberal Presbyterian, with definite assurance he was going to Hell, than a staid but, nevertheless, confused Methodist, who didn't know where the hell he was going.

This story, of course, is flexible and can be modified so as to apply effectively to any other reasonable combination of denominations, such as the Methodists and Episcopalians.

THE BISHOP OF WESTERN PENNSYLVANIA CONTRIBUTES ONE

A former Episcopal Bishop of Erie, Pennsylvania, is one of the most dynamic and interesting speakers I know. His speeches, quite aside from his sermons, always sparkle with good stories.

In a personal meeting with him he asked me to tell him one of my stories he had heard about, and on an exchange basis, he related this one:

A certain individual who was blessed with all he needed in life had little concern for or interest in his fellow men. His complete disregard for others was particularly reflected in his excessively frugal and sparing attitude about money. He was penurious to the point of being stingy and miserly about pennies. The idea of "you can't take it with you" never occurred to him. He expressed no good will whatsoever in his community. Rather unexpectedly he died. As many of his kind, he felt his monetary gain, which he had been so much concerned about in life, would assure him of an easy passage to Heaven.

St. Peter was ready for him. When he appeared at the gates of Heaven and applied for admission, St. Peter questioned him thusly: "What about your record on earth? Particularly, what have you done for your fellow men?" The man thought awhile, and finally hit upon one thing, a possible single departure from his petty nature on earth. "Why," he said, "just a few days before I died, I bought a five-cent newspaper. I gave the newsboy a dime and told him to keep the change." In doubt, St. Peter paused for a moment and then turned to the angel Gabriel and related the desire of the man to enter Heaven. Gabriel in turn asked, "What about his record; what has he done by way of good deeds on earth?" St. Peter reiterated the single instance of the man's goodwill. "He says, he bought a five-cent newspaper on earth a few days before he died and gave the newsboy a dime, and told him to keep the change."

After a brief pause Gabriel replied, "Give him a nickel, and tell him to go to Hell."

THE INQUISITIVE CLERGYMAN

Even though clergymen are concerned about their earthly needs, they subscribe to the Christian admonition: "Man cannot live by bread alone. . . ." The following story shows the concern a certain young clergyman had about the food he was going to eat before he blessed it. I have known several clergymen for whom this story had some appeal.

A young minister did not like hash. His wife acquired a French cookery book giving many recipes for using leftovers. One evening one of the fancy mixtures appeared on the table in a covered dish.

The vicar reached over and raised the cover, but his wife admonished, "Why don't you ask the blessing first, dear?"

The vicar replied: "I don't believe there is anything here that has not already been blessed."

THE EPISCOPALIANS CAN'T ESCAPE ATTENTION

Episcopalians, because of their honest liberal attitudes, make good fodder for stories. I don't know whether this story was first told by an Episcopalian, but for its inclusion here, I am indebted to the Reverend Ralph Hovencamp, rector of Trinity Episcopal Church, New Castle, Pennsylvania.

Two gentlemen, members of the Episcopal Faith, were celebrating one evening, and after showing and feeling sufficient effects of their efforts had left the place of their drinking activity, presumably for home.

Walking or ambling down the street to where they had parked their cars, they passed a small well-lighted church from which swelled the stirring tunes from well-raised voices of some old familiar hymns. Prompted by a mood for singing rather than worship, perhaps, they entered the church and took seats in a pew well forward and heartily joined in the singing with the congregation, which was completely composed of humble Negro folk, presumably Baptists.

Our two gentlemen listened to the Negro parson's sermon and when the collection plate was passed, they each contributed handsomely with a ten-dollar bill.

After the service was over, our friends had left and the parson was talking with the colored gentleman who had brought the collection plate, with the surprising contributions, about the identity of the contributors. The parson inquired, "Who were those gentlemen who put those bills in the plate, Sam?"

"Well, it was those two white gentlemen, parson."

"Yes, I know, but were they Baptists, brother?"

"All I know is when they put those ten-dollar bills in the plate, they acted mighty like Presbyterians but they smelled like Episcopalians."

A STORY ENJOYED BY TWO COLLEGE PRESIDENTS

Father Joseph Noonan, who for years was President of Niagara University, always enjoyed hearing the story of the priest intoning Mass, in which he recognized a wholesome spirit of fun and certainly no suggestion of the irreligious.

Among the repertoire of the author's stories this story was also a great favorite of the late Dr. Paul D. Moody, for many years the beloved president of Middlebury College in Vermont, and on many occasions he prevailed upon the author to tell it.

The Mass had begun and the priest had taken his position in the chancel facing the congregation and the processional, which in slow measured pace, led by youthful acolytes swinging the censers or incense pots, was coming down the church aisle. As he faced the processional, the priest began to intone the "Gloria Patri" in the typical fashion of the chant: Gloria Patri, et Filio, et Spiritui sancto, adjutorium, pax vobiscum . . . . Suddenly his voice broke off and he stopped singing the chant and looked down directly at one of the acolytes whom he noticed was not carrying the incense burner or censer. With concern the priest began to chant again. "Gloria Patri, et Filio, et Spiritui sancto, adjutorium, pax vobiscum." He this time added (still chanting), looking at the young acolyte, "What did you do with the incense pot?" to which the boy answered in the spirit and tone of the chant, "I dropped it in the aisle, it got too damn hot."

Of course, the successful telling of this story depends upon the ability to get the effect of the chant and the occasional prolonged tones peculiar to it. The effect is heightened if the response of the young acolyte is given in the falsetto voice.

The story, if well given, is always popularly received. The late Arthur Bennett Allen, who for years was a successful radio actor appearing on National Broadcasting programs with Parker Fennelly and others, delighted in telling this story.

FOR CLERGYMEN—AND CHURCHGOING LAYMEN

You probably have heard or read the little story about the minister, who at the end of the Easter service dismissed his congregation with these words:

"Since I shall most likely not see most of you until next Easter, I want to wish you, 'A Merry Christmas' now."

MORTON DOWNEY TELLS A "QUICKIE" ABOUT THE GREAT PREACHER HENRY WARD BEECHER

And Morton Downey, who heard the story, remembered a yarn concerning Dr. Henry Ward Beecher, the great preacher, . . . Dr. Beecher was told that he used poor grammar in a sermon . . . "Did I?" he said. "Well, all I have to say is—God help the grammar if it gets in my way when I'm preaching."

BISHOP SHERRILL, THE PRESIDING BISHOP OF THE EPISCOPAL CHURCH, LIKES STORIES AND CREATES ONE

Some years ago I attended the inaugural of the new president of Hobart and William Smith Colleges in New York State, at which time I had the privilege of having a very pleasant visit with the Right Reverend Henry Knox Sherrill, the presiding Bishop of the Episcopal Church. I also heard him give several talks and I was convinced he possessed a high quality of humor.

The Reverend Dr. G. Bromley Oxnam tells this story as an illustration of not only the Bishop's apparent sense of humor but also his great poise:

One Sunday when Bishop Sherrill still headed the Diocese of Massachusetts, a seedy drunk followed the churchgoers into St. Paul's Cathedral in Boston, where the Bishop was visiting and preaching on this particular day. He stood by, blinking, as the altar boys and choir marched past in the opening procession. At the end of the line, marching alone, was Bishop Sherrill, and the drunk amiably fell in beside him. The Bishop paused only to smile a welcome and proffer a much-needed arm to his lurching companion. They walked to the head of the aisle before they met a nervous usher. "This is one of your parishioners," said Bishop Sherrill, extricating his arm and walking on toward the altar.

THE ANGLICAN BISHOP'S ANNIVERSARY

A Bishop of the Anglican Church had reached the occasion of his fiftieth wedding anniversary and the friends and clergy of his diocese had made the occasion a memorable event by giving him a golden wedding anniversary party. Among the guests attending was a very attractive young French girl, who was a little confused as to the purpose and meaning of the celebration, beyond knowing it had some vague connection with marriage.

Presently she came upon the bishop. He greeted her and expressed his delight at her presence at his golden wedding anniversary party. She then replied, "Oh, yes, thees golden wedding, I do not understand—what does thees mean?"

"Well, my dear young lady," said the bishop. "It simply means I have been living with the same lady for fifty years, and . . ." Before he could continue, she responded with an element of surprise.

"Ooh! I see! You have been leeving with thees same lady for feefty years, and now you are going to marry her."

PREACHERS WHO LACK TERMINAL FACILITIES

Some of the best clergymen I know, and some of the most intelligent laymen or churchmen solidly subscribe to the idea that as far as the average sermon is concerned if a preacher can't get results in twenty to thirty minutes of preaching he better quit trying. And this holds for the average talk. Yet many sermons are too long. Too many preachers have never developed a sense of terminal facility or know when to end a sermon. And here are several stories which apply to such clergymen.

SHUT OFF THE GAS

One which particularly carries the idea is about the young newly married couple. They had set up their home where the groom had worked and attended church. To make a good start, upon returning from their honeymoon, they went to church together. As he had always sung in the choir, he sat in the chancel with members of the choir and she sat inconspicuously in the rear of the church.

The service moved along at a good pace and the clergyman started his sermon. But once he started it seemed he would never finish. As he preached on and on the young bride worried about her dinner in the oven at home. Finally she gave a note to the usher to take up to her young husband. The usher, however, handed it to the preacher, who was intent upon preaching, regardless of having been at it an hour. The preacher opened the note and read, "Hurry home and shut off the gas."

A GOOD STORY TO END A SPEECH OR A SPEECH PROGRAM

This is an especially good story for a speaker to use to end his speech or for a chairman to use to end a program. There aren't many stories suited to this important part of a speech—the end. This one, however, is ideally suited, for it insures terminal facility or ending by suggesting the audience has heard enough and it's time to go home.

A STORY USED BY A CLERGYMAN

And speaking of speakers who are long-winded and lack terminal facilities brings to mind a story of the negro who was being hunted down by the law. This story I heard told some years ago by a clergyman who came late to the alumni reunion of his college. He thought he had slipped in unnoticed by the chairman of the meeting who was on his feet introducing members of the group. He saw the clergyman and called on him for a few words, who had no desire to speak. He replied by telling the story:

In an effort to escape the police who were pursuing him, a negro criminal hurriedly entered a church and looking for a place to hide crawled up in the belfry. Everything was quiet for awhile and then he heard people moving about in the church building. For complete safety he started to crawl further up the belfry but in so doing, he slipped and started to fall. To save himself he grabbed the bell rope and pulled it down which started the bell ringing. He was immediately discovered by the church sexton, who turned him over to the police, who were pursuing him. In his disgust he looked up the belfry to the bell and said, "If it hadn't have been for your big mouth and long tongue, no one would have known I was here."

CATHOLIC OR PROTESTANT?

I don't know to whom this story must be originally ascribed, but it was first told to me by my former and beloved rector of Buffalo's Episcopal "Church of the Ascension," Dr. Charles D. Broughton, who always enjoyed a good story and possessed a fine repetoire for his own telling.

Driving one day down Buffalo's beautiful Delaware Avenue to the city in his new and first car, and being unaccustomed to the timing of the yellow light between the light change, he found himself driving through the red light. The policeman on traffic duty signaled him and approached the rector's car in a seeming irritated manner. As he put his head through the lowered car window his manner changed and apparently mistook the cleric's garb for that of a Catholic priest.

"Well, Father," he said, "you're breaking the traffic rules, my good friend, but I'll let you go this time. But let me warn you, Father, when you get to the next corner, be careful, that fellow Smith is on duty and that Protestant pup might not be so lenient with you."

ARAB STATES DELEGATE TELLS ONE

Speaking of things ecclesiastic, Dr. Ali Othman, a member of the Arab States Delegation to the United States, told this story recently to a college symposium audience.

An American in Paris was standing outside a large church amid a crowd of onlookers watching a wedding leaving the church. It seemed to be a pretty important affair so he asked a Frenchman standing near him, "Who's getting married?" The Frenchman casually replied, "Je ne sais pas."

A few days later passing the same church the American was attracted by a crowd watching a large funeral procession leaving the church. He stopped and again inquired of a Frenchman among the onlookers, "Who's being buried?" "Je ne sais pas" the Frenchman promptly replied.

The American shook his head and remarked, "Married life must have been hard on him. He certainly didn't last very long."

A STORY FOR FUND-RAISING CAMPAIGNS

A more recent rector of mine told this story to the men's organization of his church engaged in raising funds for the church development program, warning them not to be taken in by glib promises of the church members but to keep after them to sign the contribution pledge card.

It appears a member of a church conducting a similar campaign was blessed with considerable money, but he was chary about helping the church or making contributions.

He became very ill and the pastor made frequent calls upon him. Encouraged by the visits, he told the pastor if he got well he would give ten thousand dollars to the church fund.

He recovered, but refused to see the pastor on numerous calls. The clergyman finally cornered him one day on the street and pointedly reminded him, "You promised to contribute ten thousand dollars to the church fund if you got well."

"Oh, I did?" said the chary one in surprise, "That gives you an idea of how sick I was."

WHO'S CALLING THE SHOTS?

Here is a story told by the outstanding clergyman, Harry Emerson Fosdick. Prior to Dr. Fosdick's entry upon his great pastorate at The Riverside Church, New York, he had served at the Park Avenue Baptist Church in New York, which congregation moved to the new site of the Riverside Church and became the Riverside congregation.

The Park Avenue Church, planning to move, sold its property to the Central Presbyterian Church, so it was without a building. The trustees of the Temple Beth-El on Fifth Avenue offered them the use of their former synagogue, which they had just vacated for a new edifice. Fosdick relates, "Our Park Avenue congregation worshipped there until our new Riverside building was completed." He says, . . . "the courtesy and generosity of our Jewish hosts knew no bounds. One of our trustees was so moved by this exhibition of good will that meeting a friend of his, a member of Temple Emanu-El, he exclaimed, 'that was a very generous thing you did in offering us the use of your synagogue;' and then forgetting himself he added, 'That was a Christian thing to do.' 'Christian!' said his friend, 'What do you mean—"Christian?" That was a Jewish thing to do.' "

LET'S NOT BE PROVINCIAL

There certainly should be opportunity for speakers to use this story. We become circumscribed and most provincial in our views and are not sufficiently vicarious in respect to the other person's interests and viewpoint. This is a common, universal trait and evidences of it constantly appear, which speakers should be able to recognize.

THE EFFICACY OF PRAYER

The subject of prayer may quite logically fit into this section concerned with things religious.

It is St. Paul's admonition to pray without ceasing. Here is a story of a young chap, but with no thought of irreverence, who thought he had prayed enough.

He was a lonesome little fellow because he had no brother or sister and he constantly asked his father and mother why he couldn't have a baby sister or brother. His father said maybe some day he would have and told him, in the meantime, to keep on praying for one, which he agreed to do.

Finally one day the father told the little chap he wanted to take him some place as he had a surprise for him. He took him to the hospital where the boy's mother was confined. They went in the mother's room and lifted the covers on one side of the bed and the father showed the chap a little baby boy and said, "There! Aren't you happy? There's a little baby brother."

The child was extremely happy, taking it all in when the father added, "That isn't all; come with me."

He took the little fellow around to the other side of the bed, lifted the covers and showed him a second baby boy and added, "And there is another little baby brother. Now aren't you glad you prayed?"

The boy looked up into his father's face, and said, "Aren't you glad I stopped praying?"

This story is not especially appropriate to use in relation to prayer, but more particularly when or where babies are profuse.

I heard it used once when the baby production among a college faculty was quite high. The wife of one young professor had presented him with two sets of twins in successive births in almost successive years. The wife of one of his associates presented her husband with child number nine. I don't remember whether the situation affected general salary increments or not.

A STRANGE ANOMALY

Here is a case of a woman who enjoyed her pastor's sermons, but, unknowingly, wished he would soon die. At that she was more gracious than many people who wish some preachers and speakers were dead so they wouldn't have to listen to their sermons or talks.

In this vein clergymen and speakers may find interesting use for the story.

An elderly admiring female member of a congregation stopped to speak to the minister at the close of service one Sunday morning.

"Reverend, I thought you ought to know that I come to these services only because of your sermons. They are wonderful and you ought to have them published in a book."

"Oh, I don't know. I am not sure that my sermons deserve that much attention. Perhaps, some day, they will be published posthumously."

Woman (enthusistically): "Well, then, I hope that will be real soon."

CHAPTER NINE

About Englishmen—
the British, Scotch and Irish
Some Comments

. . . Rare compound of oddity, frolic and fun!
Who relished a joke, and rejoiced in a pun.
—Goldsmith

The Englishman is the butt and target of many American stories because of his tendency to garble the point of the story and his further slow comprehension of the American brand of humor.

In this latter connection it has been remarked, "Don't ever tell a story to an Englishman on a Saturday night, because there is the danger he will laugh Sunday morning in church."

GOVERNOR DEWEY AND LOWELL THOMAS ENJOYED THIS STORY OF AN ENGLISHMAN

A prominent Presbyterian clergyman in Central New York is the Reverend Ralph Lankler. Dr. Lankler also serves as summer pastor of the interesting Community Church at Pawling, New York, which former Governor Dewey and Lowell Thomas attend. They are friends of the clergyman, and I am certain they have enjoyed hearing him tell this story which is one of his favorites.

An Englishman had been in the United States for a considerable time and because of the press of business he had completely forgotten the request of his British friends to bring back a good American story. On the day he was making his departure from America, as he was checking out at the Astor Hotel, he realized that he did not have one good story to take back to his friends in England. With the hope that something might still be done, he asked the clerk at the Astor if he could tell him a story that he could take to his friends.

The clerk said he didn't know a story, but he could tell him a riddle which might interest him.

"A riddle?" said the Englishman. "Oh . . . I'm sure that will do right well."

The clerk began. "A child was born to my mother and father. Now he is not my brother and he is not my sister. Who is he?"

The Englishman, with a perplexed look, thought a moment and said, "Oh, my! I'm sure I don't know." To which the clerk replied, "Why, it is I."

"Oh, my! Quite good, eh what?" said the Englishman.

Upon returning home and being asked to tell a story from America, the Englishman said he couldn't tell a story, but he knew a first-rate riddle. And thus he began:

"Now let me see. A certain man and woman gave birth to a child. It wasn't male, and it wasn't female. Who was it?" His friends who were listening looked somewhat bewildered and gave no reply.

"Cawn't you get it? Give up, eh?" interrupted the Englishman. "Why, it was the clerk* at the Astor!" With a good laugh, he concluded, "Jolly good, eh what?"

AT THE OTHER END OF THE SCALE

The Englishman as typified in the above story may be a stage caricature or purely fictional. To offset this character creation, we all know Englishmen who are keen and of ready wit. The chap with whom the following story is concerned is the sort who gives promise of having a ready comprehension of the humorous story and little likelihood of garbling the point of a story.

In anticipation of the arrival of a new baby at his home, an English boy of nine was taken off for a visit with his aunt and uncle. Assuming the child was unaware of the coming blessed event, his relatives enthusiastically coveted the opportunity to break the news to the little chap.

* (The Englishman would pronounce clerk, "clark.")

With several friends gathered at the home the child's aunt thought the occasion was suitable for the telling. She was, of course, anxious to advise him about the expected arrival (the new baby) in a manner that was in keeping with a child's knowledge of such things. "Bertie," she said, "a very large stork has been seen lately, flying over the homes of your neighborhood. Of course, in some homes it has caused considerable confusion and excitement; it may be . . ." At this point little Bertie interrupted, "A large stork, you say, in our neighborhood? Oh, I do hope it doesn't frighten Mother. She's pregnant, you know."

AN ENGLISH STORY ON PRONUNCIATION

Speakers and Pronunciation

Speakers are concerned about pronunciation because often when speaking they have misgivings about how to pronounce words. Certain localities and places have pronunciations peculiar to the area; provincialisms they are called. Quincy may be Quin' zee, or Quince' see; Kearney becomes Carney, and there are many variations. Various areas of our states have a disturbing breakdown of names into peculiar local dialect which really concerns the speaker who travels much. It isn't easy for the speaker. In spite of standardized pronunciation of English, area pronunciations prevail.

Some names and places, however, are correct only one way and must be respected for their established and proper pronunciation. For instance, Sault Sainte Marie is pronounced Soo Sainte Marie; Worcester is Wooster, viscount is vi-count and any variance of these is charged to ignorance.

Of course, anyone may be allowed a mistake or two, but a good speaker should keep abreast of pronunciation, or he isn't a speaker. If one is good enough, he may express a reasonable indifference to such matters as the great Dr. Henry Ward Beecher did when he was criticized for grammar errors in his preaching. He said, "When I'm preaching the gospel of the Lord, if the English grammar gets in my way, God help it."

If such details of the language as pronunciation bother one too much, he shouldn't attempt to speak or even tell stories. In other words he can do as the American in London does in this story, just give up.

PREFERS HIS ENGLISH IN AMERICA

After the war an American spending some time in London was having a difficult time with the British pronunciations. It was bad enough to learn that clerk was pronounced clark; Berkeley was pronounced Barkeley and lieutenant was pronounced leftenant. But when he saw a marquee on a picture house which read, *A Revival of Cavalcade: Pronounced Success*, "That settles it," he said, "I'm going home."

SPEAKING OF PRONUNCIATION

This story, originally in slightly different form, and in dialect other than good English, is ascribed to Harry Hershfield, one of our best known modern storytellers.

An English chap entered a drugstore and said to the pharmacist, "I need some medicine, but I've lost the prescription."

"I cawn't help you unless you can remember the name of the medicine."

The Englishman thought for a moment and said, "As I remember, it sounds like one of our large cities." And then slowly he continued, "London—Manchester—Birmingham—Liverpool, Ah, that's it! Carter's Little Liverpools."

TWO ENGLISH BISHOPS

This story has humor even though with somewhat of an ironical twist. But clergymen should delight in telling it, or other speakers should enjoy telling it about clergymen. It can be adapted to special speaking occasions, but because it possesses the elements of a good story it has broad general use.

Two Anglican bishops who had spent fifty years in the Church died and went up to Heaven expecting an easy and direct passage through the gates guarded by St. Peter and his staff. One of the attendants, however, said the bishops would have to wait in a reception room until their records and background were checked.

Just as they were about to go into the reception room a young attractive blonde entered, approached St. Peter, exchanged a few words, presented a paper which St. Peter examined and then passed her through the gates into Heaven.

The bishops seeing all this were surprised and a little disturbed because of the blonde's prompt admittance into Heaven.

They immediately approached St. Peter and questioned him as to why the blonde was promptly allowed to enter the gates to Heaven, when they, who had spent fifty years in the service of the Lord, were being held up.

"Why," St. Peter answered, "this young blonde we just let go through the gates had a beautiful high-powered car when she was down on earth, but the way she drove that car! Why, she sent us more business than the two of you have been able to do in the fifty years you've been working at it."

WHERE AM I?

Gene Raymond, the actor, has told a modified version of this story. It has to do with a situation of bewilderment quite often well revealed by the Englishman. A speaker often finds himself in a similar situation and the story might well be used for such an occasion.

Two British actors were appearing in a Shakespearian play. Some members of the audience, reverting to the days of Elizabethan drama, became unruly. One of the actors spoke to them, which caused the other actor to forget his lines so he started to ad lib. The ad libbing disturbed the other actor and, as a result, he began to ad lib. They kept this up for some time when suddenly they stopped, being unable to think of anything to say.

Then one actor in desperation finally said, "The line? the line? Oh, what is the line?" Looking surprised and bewildered the other one replied, "The line, what is the line? Oh, I say, what is the play?"

ANOTHER CONFUSED BRITISHER

We are indebted to Bennett Cerf for this story, which seems like a good one to include as an example of the Englishman who speaks without thinking of the possible implication. Here again the idea may apply to the speaker and the speaking situation.

From India comes the story of the rather gay old colonel who was pretty well up in his seventies. He startled his associates and the community by marrying a beautiful chic girl of nineteen. As the story goes, a year later she presented him with an eight-pound son. The overjoyed colonel assembled the entire regiment, mounted the bandstand, cleared his throat and announced, "I have called you all together to tell you that my wife gave birth this morning to a strapping baby boy. Gentlemen, I thank you."

BRING IN THE AMERICAN COUNTERPART

This story only finds a place because humor, which seems peculiar to the Englishman, is common to the American. As far as its application to a speech situation the story is self-explanatory.

The story appeared in "Clever Introductions For Chairmen," published by T. S. Denison & Company, and is supposed to have been told by the actor Bill Powell. Here it is.

I looked forward to the honor of introducing to you tonight the famed economist, Dr. Harold S. Doakes. Mr. Doakes, I am certain, would have given a splendid talk had he been able to attend. When the illustrious gentleman did not arrive on the morning train from Chicago, I became alarmed, so I called him long distance for an explanation.

He apologized profusely and said that he was unable to come to Swanville as he met up with a heart-rending situation at the Union Station, just as he was about to board the train. It appears that an elderly woman in dire distress was trying to secure sleeping accommodations on the train, for the purpose of going to a son who was dangerously ill. The train was sold out so Dr. Doakes obligingly gave up his ticket. The good doctor concluded his telephone conversation with me by saying, "I sent you a telegram giving the details."

This afternoon I received the wire which reads, "Regret will not be able to keep speaking engagement. Gave berth to an elderly lady last night."

MR. BRITAIN'S WIT A MATCH FOR THE IRISH WIT— GEORGE BERNARD SHAW

During a period in Churchill's life when his political stock was down the Irish wit and playwright, George Bernard Shaw, thought it would be an ideal time to direct a shaft at the prime minister with the ever-present thought that it would react to his own glory. It reacted in the manner of a boomerang.

The occasion was the approaching premiere performance of a new play of Shaw's. He wrote to Churchill telling him a play he had just completed was soon to be given its first performance at a London theater and he would like to have the statesman attend. The playwright added he would be very happy to include an extra ticket for a friend, if Churchill had a friend.

Churchill lost no time in acknowledging the gracious offer of the renowned Shaw and he replied to the playwright's added crack about bringing a friend with a completely devastating one. He said he would be unable to avail himself of the kind offer to witness the first performance of the play, but he would be glad to come to the second performance, if the play had a second performance.

There was the Englishman who reported his conversation with the American in respect to the main difference in becoming King of England and President of the United States.

"Let me see," began the Englishman "the American chap said, 'To become King of England you have to be the son of your father, but in order to become President of the United States, you don't have to be the son of your father. You can be the son of anybody's father.' "

BERNARD SHAW'S MODESTY

That brilliant Irishman, George Bernard Shaw, was considered, during his lifetime, somewhat conceited by many people. In reality he was a modest man. Shaw was born at 33 Synge Street, Dublin. When it was decided to place a tablet on the Shavian birthplace, many inscriptions embodying words of high praise were suggested. Finally Shaw was asked what he would like on the tablet. He suggested the following, which now can be seen on the side of the house: "Bernard Shaw, author of many plays, was born in this house, 26th July, 1856.

COMPLETING THE BRITISH ISLES

Stories about any part of the British Isles are not complete without including all the groups, so included here are stories about the Irish and Scotch.

Here is a story about the Irish reportedly told by Arthur Godfrey:

It seems three brothers who came to this country from Ireland several years ago had all made good in a fantastic way.

On their mother's 75th birthday, each decided to outdo the others in the lavishness of his gift to her. One son sent her a beautiful car, complete with the services of a chauffeur. Another sent her a coat of the finest mink available. The third son, striving for something completely out of the ordinary, located a talking parrot — one whose vocabulary boasted several thousand words, all in the Gaelic tongue.

At the party, after many speeches of congratulations, the boys took their mother aside.

"Well, Mither," said one, "How did you like the car?"

"Ah!" exclaimed the woman. "It's beautiful—and so luxurious."

"And the coat?" asked the second.

"I am the envy of everyone!" exclaimed the mother.

"And the bird—what did you think of it?" cried the third son.

"Ah—it was wonderful!" exclaimed the woman. "Simply delicious."

IRISH LOGIC

Two Irishmen met on the street and rushed up to shake hands. At the same moment each discovered he was unacquainted with the other. "Beg your pardon—" began one.

"Faith, and it's all right," said the other, "you see I thought it was you, and you thought it was me, and bejabers, it wasn't either of us!"

SCOTCH THRIFT

Sandy McTavish loved to play golf, but one bright day his friends saw him sitting forlornly in the club house without his golf clubs.

"Why aren't you out on the course playing golf, Sandy?" said one of his friends.

"Aye, I nae can play agin," said Sandy disconsolately.

"Why not?" asked the friend.

"Aye," said Sandy, "I lost me ball."

ANOTHER ONE

Another typical Scotch story is about the Scotch chemistry professor who was demonstrating the properties of various acids.

"Now please pay careful attention," he said.

"I am going to drop this two shilling piece into this glass of acid. Will it dissolve?"

"No, sir," spoke up one student promptly.

"No?" said the professor. "Will you explain to the class why it won't dissolve?"

"Because," said the student, "if it would, you wouldn't drop it in."

NO SECOND CHANCE

Jock Malcolm of Scotland was invited by a friend of his to come down to London for a visit and look over the great metropolis.

Jock arrived in London and his friend met him at the railway station. Somewhat surprised at seeing Jock alone his friend approached him and asked, "Where's your wife, Jock? Why didn't you bring her along to enjoy the sights?"

"Oh, I couldna' bring Daisy. She's already been to London."

The deft speaker, of course, fully realizes that there are numerous occasions and possibilities to use such Scotch stories as these. The real advantage of their use, however, lies in the value of association with human relations and situations. They do not necessarily have the limited value of revealing a commonly accepted Scotch trait.

ALL ITEMS CONSIDERED

The installment plan is so universal among Americans that it can humorously be applied by speakers to a most important phase of life, life itself. It should have varied use in speeches.

MacDougal, the Scot, kept a budget; and he especially prized his new baby a few weeks old. He had just received his pay check for the month and he was at his desk going over his expenses and making out his budget. He itemized his accounts aloud as follows: "Rent—fifty dollars; Groceries—seventy-five dollars; Fuel—twenty dollars; Miscellaneous—thirty dollars; Medical"—and then after a studied pause, he yelled, "Hurrah! One more payment and the baby's ours."

THE DIFFERENCE AMONG THE ENGLISH, SCOTTISH, AND IRISH

And now correlating the three groups by citing this difference. It is said when an Irishman is leaving a train, he walks off without looking to see whether he has left anything behind; an Englishman looks back to see if he has left anything; and a Scotchman looks back to see whether anybody else has left anything.

THE PEOPLE OF THE BRITISH ISLES

Here is some interesting commentary about the people of the British Isles made by Dr. Henry M. Wriston, former President of Brown University, when speaking before a group of college students. It has valuable application for many groups of a cosmopolitan make-up when differences must be reconciled for understanding.

Dr. Wriston said, "The Bishop of Birmingham on one occasion was making a speech to a group of railroad men in England. He said, 'You have done a wonderful thing. You have gotten four nationalities to understand each other—the Englishman, who loves his Bible and his beer, the Scotchman, who keeps the Sabbath and anything else he can lay his hands on, the Welshman, who prays on Sunday and on his neighbors the rest of the week, and the Irishman, who doesn't know what he wants but will never be happy until he gets it.' " *

*Adapted from THE MASTER GUIDE FOR SPEAKERS, T. S. Denison and Company.

CHAPTER TEN

From the Entertainment World

I cannot tell how the truth may be;
I say the tale as 't was said to me.
—Scott

As previously pointed out, the sources for the humorous story are multiple and among them must be included the several phases of the field of entertainment.

Perhaps the stories are not to be derived from the various media of entertainment as much as from the personalities engaged in these various media, the actors or people themselves.

The stories included here are about personalities of the entertainment field. The stories may be adaptible to speeches or speech material, but in a sense they may have special use because of their intrinsic story value and may be used independently.

Several of them are not the run-of-the-mill type of story and have interesting reading as well as telling value. Whenever they are told, they presuppose good interpretation by the teller.

LAURETTE TAYLOR, A FAMOUS AMERICAN ACTRESS, LIKE MANY PERFORMERS HAD A FINE SENSE OF HUMOR

Some years ago in the American Theater perhaps the best known impersonator was a chap named Albert Carroll.

Theatergoers who reached their maturity in the middle twenties will recall Carroll's impersonations of theatrical figures in the sparkling *Grand Street Follies* presented by the Neighborhood Playhouse, New York. At the end of each theatrical season it was the impish custom of this group to pick apart the Broadway year and deftly caricature the more eventful plays and players.

Carroll was the mainstay of these frolics and his impersonations were startlingly accurate. In appearance, voice, and mannerisms, he was even more like the originals than the originals themselves. As James Cagney says, as he walks into a scene of a recent picture and sees someone impersonating him, "One of us must be terrible." Not so with Carroll.

In 1924 Carroll impersonated Pavlowa, Irene Castle, and John Barrymore in "The Jest," among others. He reached outside the theater and did the then Prince of Wales and Barrymore again when he did "Hamlet." After a performance Barrymore attended, Carroll recalls the actor wrote him: "This is not only the best impersonation I've ever seen but it's fine creative work. If you ever play Hamlet seriously, there'll be nothing for me to do but impersonate you."

The Follies was a seasonal event for the uptown Broadway theatrical world and most of the stars impersonated went down to the Neighborhood Playhouse to see themselves as others saw them. They included Joseph Schildkraut, Lynn Fontainne, Gertrude Lawrence, Constance Collier, Laurette Taylor, Minnie Maddern Fiske, Ethel Barrymore and those already named.

To gather material for his impersonations, Carroll used to spend weeks in Broadway theaters, watching the performers at work. Most of them were anxious to give him pointers.

He recalls that while he was studying Laurette Taylor appearing in Zoe Atkins, "The Furies," he was backstage for every performance, and she was gracious and helpful. When he had finally left, Miss Taylor was seen shaking out her white chiffon gown before going on the stage. Her co-performer, who was that fine actress Estelle Winwood said, "What's the matter, Laurette? Is there anything wrong with your dress?"

"No," replied Miss Taylor. "I just wanted to make sure Albert Carroll wasn't in it."

A TWIN BILL IS CONFUSING

Recently a movie entitled, "You Can't Beat The Irish," was playing at a Park Avenue theater in New York. This picture was made in Ireland and all the characters in this picture spoke with an Irish brogue. Also, on the same bill at the same theater was the picture, "Faithful City," a story about Israel.

An old Jewish couple came into the theater as the Irish picture was about half over. Apparently, they came to see the one about Israel and thought that this was the middle of it. After about ten minutes of Irish dialect the old lady turned to her husband and pointedly inquired:

"That's the way they speak in Palestine?"

WALTER WINCHELL REPORTS

Walter Winchell reports that one of his celebrity friends says the only reason he goes to the movies is to keep his friends from telling him about them . . . I like that one about Wilson Mizner, who had a shopkeeper pal—and they both enjoyed kidding each other. One day a panhandler walked into the shop and asked for a handout . . . "Ask him," said the shopkeeper, "he's the boss" . . . The bum told Mizner a long story . . . Mizner put on his hat and started walking out. At the door he turned to the real owner and said: "Okay, give him $1 from the till."

Take it from Walter Winchell which is how we got it. Winchell relates that Bing Crosby nurses two newspaper clippings, which he prizes highly. One is a review of his first movie in which he played the lead, but his name is not recorded once in the entire notice.

The second clipping is a review of a picture which starred a rival crooner. It says in part: "Russ Columbo has a fine voice, but he can't act as well as Bing Crosby, who can't act at all!"

A FAVORITE STORY OF WILL ROGERS

Certainly one good evidence of immortality, or what may be expressed as the overtones of great souls who have passed on, is recounting little stories and anecdotes that they always cherished.

A return to the great spirit and vibrant personality of the late Will Rogers is always brought forth when one of his favorite stories is recalled.

Some years ago in a small town out West, the one and only hotel was chocked full of guests, when two salesmen arrived lookin' for accommodations for the night. The proprietor couldn't squeeze them in any place and was about to turn them away when he remembered an old church across the street which he had bought intending to add it to his establishment. Since there was no other place in town to sleep that night he had a pretty easy job convincing the new arrivals that they ought to spend the night in this building.

All was well in the quiet little town until about midnight when the church bell began to ring out clear and loud. After a while the night clerk woke up and shaking the sleepy bellhop, sent him out to investigate. The clerk waited a couple of minutes when the boy ran in and chirped, "The man in pew sixteen was ringing for gingerale."

A PROFESSIONAL ACTOR PATRONIZES THE AMATEURS

Herbert Marshall, at a dinner in Hollywood, sat beside a beautiful young lady, an amateur actress from Chicago.

"We gave several amateur plays before I left home last week," the girl said. "They were just splendid, too."

She looked at Mr. Marshall and frowned thoughtfully. Then she added:

"The only trouble was that the audience would laugh in the wrong place."

"My dear young lady," said Mr. Marshall, "there is no such thing as laughing in the wrong place in amateur theatricals."

ANOTHER ACTRESS TELLS A STORY

Shirley Booth, the leading lady of "A Tree Grows in Brooklyn," and champion actress (according to recent polls), tells it herself, her favorite story. . . . She knew that her former groom, Ed Gardner (Archie), was fickle and couldn't be depended on to stay faithful—but she loved him very much and married him. On their honeymoon cruise to the Caribbean, he suddenly said: "I'm going for a stroll around the deck," and out he went. Shirley suspected he had seen something on board and was out hunting. An hour later she decided to take a stroll, too. As she turned a corner, their eyes clashed. He was coming out of a cabin when his wife nailed him. "Oh, all right," he sulked. "Now you know. I'm a jewel thief!"

A SANTA CLAUS STORY FROM A FORMER
MOVIE ACTRESS

One of the darlings of the silent movies who was one of the sweetest and most beautiful personalities to have graced the screen or the stage in the last fifty years was Lillian "Dimples" Walker. I am sure she is still a sweet and attractive person.

Back in the roaring twenties when Buffalo was dedicating one of its finer cinema theaters Lillian appeared with Kenneth Harlan, another silent movie idol, and other stars of the day, at a civic banquet held in conjunction with the dedication ceremonies.

Her beauty alone enhanced the occasion but in her sweet inimitable way, Miss Walker further proved her value with a good speech and a few stories.

The occasion was held very close to the Christmas Holiday season and Lillian Walker told the following gay, but not too risque Santa Claus story, which coming from this attractive lady especially pleased the audience.

On Christmas Eve little Mary, visiting with her parents and her favorite Aunt Mary, had expressed an enthusiasm— the desire to stay up so she might watch for, and possibly see, Santa Claus. But her parents, encouraging her with the belief that sometime she would see Santa Claus at work, put her to bed. In anticipation of Santa's visit she had for the time fallen asleep, a happy child.

In the morning she was welcomed by her Auntie's Christmas greeting and the remark that Santa had been and left a beautiful tree surrounded by so many gifts. Mary said yes, she knew about Santa's visit as she had seen him last night from her bed.

Being interested her aunt said, "You did? Well, tell Auntie about it."

"Well," Mary began, "I was looking from my bed when I saw Santa come in this room. I got up and watched him. He trimmed the tree; then he put all the gifts around the tree."

"Yes," said her aunt still interested.

"And then," Mary said, "after he had put all the gifts around, I watched him and *he went and got in bed with Mama.*"

FROM GEORGE ABBOTT THE THEATRICAL PRODUCER

A news bureau writer reports this little anecdote as coming from George Abbott, the prominent and efficent New York theatrical producer. Abbott has been associated with the Broadway scene as actor, director and producer for over thirty-five years. His successes as producer include, *Three Men on a Horse, Room Service, Brother Rat,* and more recently *The Pajama Game* and *Damn Yankees.*

A reporter was asking Abbott whether he always had the same backers or angels for his shows, hinting to the producer he might like to put a little money into a production. He added, "That is an investment I have never tried, but it would be fun to have a nodding acquaintance with the stage doorman and be able to walk in behind the scenes, and perhaps mingle with the actors."

In his usual quiet spoken manner Abbott's answer reflected no enthusiasm for the reporter being a backer or having any other association with his productions.

The reporter revealed in his reply that he sensed the producer's feeling.

"Don't you get tired of people like me always asking questions about show business?" he said. "It's like a doctor who can get a lot of volunteer patients at a dinner or cocktail party."

"Yes," answered Abbott and clinched his distaste for talking shop by adding this little story.

"Reminds me of a fellow who was introduced to a doctor at some social affair. He began to talk medicine. Then he got around to his own symptoms.

" 'You know,' he said, 'I have had a pain in my upper left side for about a week. It starts here. Have you any idea what causes it?' He pointed to the spot.

" 'But I'm a Ph.D.,' he was answered, 'specializing in investments for a banking house.'

" 'Well, Doc, have you got any good tips on the stock market?' "

The above story may not find a use by a medical doctor, but it is ideally suited for an economist or educator who has a Ph.D. Of course, it can be adapted by others for speaking occasions.

ABOUT ACTORS AND JOHN BARRYMORE

During the depression of the thirties an idle actor sat in the lobby of an off-Broadway hotel with a friend and bemoaned the lack of work in the theater.

"Do you know," he said, "it is reported there are five thousand actors walking Broadway?" To which the friend casually replied, "Who said they were actors?"

And, of course, it may have been that some of them would never have found work in the theater if they waited until doomsday; yet unless they starved they were going to act before they went to work—at something else, if it presented itself.

It is not to be implied that the business of acting doesn't entail the possibility of work, but it can be said that some actors, when need be, are reluctant to leave the theater's realm of illusion for the realistic work world or for another job. For them such associations are disdainful.

In his story of John Barrymore, *Good Night Sweet Prince*, Gene Fowler reveals no particular aversion to work on the part of "the Great Profile," but Barrymore's uncle, John Drew, on one occasion, did.

It was in 1906—the year of the "San Francisco Earthquake," or more commonly known in "Frisco" as the "big fire." According to his uncle, John Barrymore was playing the town. He was asleep about three in the morning when the event occurred. The shock that hit his hotel landed with such force that it knocked John out of bed. Before he was able to get his bearings he had landed in the bathtub. He crawled to his feet, put on some clothes, and started to walk to town through the rubble.

By this time the Army had taken charge. As the actor came along, a soldier jabbed a bayonet into the seat of his pants and handed him a pickax with instructions to pitch in.

Commenting on the actor's experience, John Drew remarked:

"Well, it took a convulsion of nature to get Jack into the bathtub and the United States Army to put him to work."

———————

I recently heard a speaker use this story in an effective way, revealing the lethargy on the part of most people in getting things done. He explained that getting action on some things is like attempting to move heaven and earth and too often serious awakenings must occur first.

FROM THE ACTOR CHARLES COBURN

Charles Coburn, the movie actor and erstwhile legitimate theater actor and, some years ago, producer at the Coburn

Theater in New York, must have had an early interest in the theater. He relates that when he was very young his father warned him about the evils of certain types of theaters.

"What kind of theaters, Father?" he asked.

"Burlesque theaters, son. Don't ever go in one."

"Why not?" he promptly asked.

"Because you'll see things in a burlesque theater that you shouldn't see," his father answered.

This aroused Coburn's curiosity.

"Not too long after," he relates, "I took in my first burlesque show. Whenever I tell this story," he adds, "someone always asks, 'And did you see something you shouldn't have seen?' "

"I have to laugh when I answer, 'You bet I did. I saw my father.' "

SOME STORIES TOLD IN VAUDEVILLE

A lady, confined to her home because of illness, was quite perturbed by her inability to get out and take advantage of the bargains being offered in one of the town's better department stores. Rather than completely forego the opportunity she decided, as the next best thing, to send her husband on the important shopping project. She explained to him in detail the merchandise articles he was to purchase.

But with a final admonition she made a lingering impression upon the mind of her husband.

"And now, for heaven's sake, Henry, remember, if you ever expect to get up to the counter and get these things for me—be sure and act like a lady!"

A YOUNG MAN WHO ALWAYS ACTED THAT WAY

I always remember one of our better vaudeville performers of yesteryear of the Al Jolson type, but I can't recall the particular performer, who used to tell this story:

A certain man was train caller at the New York Central station in upstate Syracuse, New York. Standing at the waiting room entrance to the trains, he would pick up his megaphone and call out each train as it arrived and departed, with the gusto and volume becoming a man.

"Train number 5 for Chicago—on track number 3, stopping at Rochester, Buffalo, Erie, Cleveland, Toledo, Elkhart and Chicago, Train number 5—track number 3."

Often seated beside him was an aesthetic looking young man, who was the train caller's nephew. Whenever the train caller announced the trains, the young man seemed to revel in almost girlish delight and unbecoming the normal virility of a young man. His enthusiasm suggested that he wanted to take over the megaphone and do the calling.

Unexpectedly the train caller became ill, and there in his place in the station was the refined looking nephew. Aside from a uniform he was rather fastidiously dressed. He looked all set, ready to exhibit himself and do the train calling in a dramatic manner.

He stepped forward with the grace of a ballet dancer to call the first train. He raised the megaphone rather effeminately, and with an affected and subdued voice began:

"Train number 15 for the east—track 4, stopping at Utica, Albany, Poughkeepsie, and New York."

He turned and walked toward the entrance to the trains

and stopped abruptly as a train was heard rumbling through on the tracks.

He turned toward the passengers, ran daintily in their direction and raising his hands effeminately, disgustedly intoned,

"Oh, girls! It's my mistake; it's nothing but a nasty old freight train."

Telling this story may have little value beyond the idea of a story for story's sake. Even then it requires good interpretation and some element of impersonation to suggest an effeminate person. In other words, it is not material to be used by the average speaker to illustrate a point or an idea.

A STORY WHICH ILLUSTRATES BEING IN THE SAME BOAT

Very often a speaker wishes to point out that due to circumstances members of his audience must recognize that they have all been placed in the same or analogous position. Juxtaposition is the ideal word, which literally means placed side by side or parallel. Here is a delightful story which is admirably suited to point this out:

I first heard it told by a monologist who attributed it to Bennett Cerf; so it may be said to come from television where he constantly appears. It may have appeared in one of his humorous story volumes.

Slotkin and Reuben were both well established in the garment or ready-to-wear business—Slotkin in New York and Reuben in Chicago.

Each was required to take a trip to the other's city and it happened they decided to travel at the same time. Slotkin left New York for Chicago on the same day that Reuben left Chicago for New York.

Being aristocrats in the garment trade they always traveled first class. This time they both boarded the Central's crack Twentieth Century Limited for their respective destinations.

The two crack trains, as the story goes, reached Buffalo at the same time and Slotkin and Reuben met while strolling the platform during the stop. They became so engrossed in conversation that without thinking they both boarded the eastbound train.

Sometime later, Slotkin suddenly stopped talking in the middle of the conversation and said, "Reuben! Have you ever stopped to think what a wonderful age this is we live in?"

"Exactly what do you mean?" asked Reuben, somewhat disinterestedly. "Well, take today for instance," said Slotkin thoughtfully. "Here, you are going from Chicago to New York; and I am going from New York to Chicago—and we're both on the same train."

HOBBIES

The engagement of an actor to a pretty young starlet was announced recently at a Hollywood party.

"Well, she's a fine girl," said a friend, "she'll make him a good first wife."

Jan Sterling, the actress, was being interviewed and when questions about her plays and her career seemed to have been satisfied, the interviewer turned to interrogating her about her husband, the actor, Paul Douglas.

After a few routine questions, the interviewer, somewhat pointedly, said, "Does your husband, Paul, have any special hobby?"

"Does he have any special hobby?" came back Jan Sterling's quick response. "After all, I am his third wife."

SUCH IS FAME

This little story points up the truth of the Biblical quotation, that a man is not without honor except in his own home and his own country.

Johnny Marks, Colgate University of the class of '31 and a songwriter, has given us some fine tunes and has entertained with his own compositions on both the Ed Sullivan and Gene Autry Shows and has appeared on "What's My Line?"

Perhaps his latest released work by his own publishing firm is "I Heard the Bells on Christmas Day." There have been many others, but the one upon which his fame rests is the song written in 1949 and introduced at Madison Square Garden by Gene Autry, "Rudolph, the Red-Nosed Reindeer," the unique history and popularity of which is without precedent.

The Colgate University *Alumni News*, reports that Johnny lives with his wife and their three children in New York's Greenwich Village. One day Michael, 7, came home from school and begged his mother to buy him a record of the red-nosed reindeer song everybody was singing. Such is fame!

VIVE LE—NEW YORK BOYS

This title seems to suggest a language hybrid, but in idiom form excellently conveys the thought for which it is used in this amusing story.

This little tale which actually was told on television has its obvious use in connection with romantic ideas, but certainly could be well used for more practical and prosaic purposes.

A most attractive young lady recently appeared on the television program, *Name That Tune.* In the usual questioning by the emcee, the amiable George DeWitt, she revealed she was unmarried and came from Alabama. He suggested that he was certain she was kept busy by the young men in Manhattan, to which she only mildly responded.

He then asked her if she liked dating the boys better at home or the New York boys, and in what respect did their romantic habits or manners differ.

"Well," she answered, "when I date the boys in my Alabama home town, they all know me and their manner is more gracious. They take me out and they do not try to kiss me the first time, because they know they will see me again tomorrow or tomorrow. In other words there is always a tomorrow.

"But in New York, when I go out with boys the way they act they give me the impression that tomorrow will never come."

HEARD ON RED SKELTON'S PROGRAM

All young men aren't like the New York boys.

"Red" Skelton tells about the chap who was visiting his girl one evening, just sitting and telling her how much he loved her and calling her pet names. He said,

"You know, my darling, sometimes I wish I were built like an octopus and had eight arms so I could just love you with all eight of them."

"Yeah," said his girl friend, "What's the matter with making use of the two you've got?"

AN ACTRESS—ON COLLEGE BOYS' LOVE MAKING

Margie Hart, the actress whom they say outstrips (i.e. at the box office) the famed Gypsy Rose Lee, must have had some romantic experience with boys of the traditionally big three of the Ivy League. She says:

"Harvard men are always gentlemen.

"And you can always have a good long talk with a Princeton man.

"But based on my experience with Yale men, I wonder if they teach anything there but blocking and tackling."

A STORY FROM THE FAMOUS ALGONQUIN HOTEL

One day in the "thirties" I sat at luncheon in New York's Algonquin Hotel with a group of actors. Irvin Cobb, the humorist, who like many talented folks belonged to the Algonquin coterie, was just leaving the dining room which occasioned a story about him and Fannie Hurst by one of the group.

Fannie Hurst, the writer, acquired a beautiful figure by rigorous and faithful diet. It appears, one day, Irvin Cobb followed her down Fifth Avenue for about six blocks without recognizing her. Finally she called to him and said, "aren't you going to speak to me, Irvin?"

"Good Lord!" said Cobb, taking a good look at her. "Fannie Hurst, the same old Fannie!"

"The same Fannie Hurst," she agreed, "quite true, but not the same Fannie."

THE GAY OR RISQUE STORY

These anecdotes are about as gay as the volume includes, and maybe a little risque for some audiences. Such stories may not be suitable for women's groups and then again the ladies may cherish a little spice.

I talked before a women's group one time and in advance I was instructed to let my hair down and tell a few gay stories as their husbands would attend the meeting. So I told them this story:

REPUTATION STILL RESPECTABLE

A dignified maiden lady hurried from the elevator to the desk of a San Francisco hotel and indignantly said to the clerk, "I thought this was a respectable hotel."

To which the clerk answered, "I thought so too. Is there something wrong?"

The lady answered, "Yes, I just got off the elevator on my floor and a marine was chasing a young lady, clad in her negligée, down the hall."

The clerk mused for a minute then looked at and leaned over to the lady and said, "Did he catch her?"

"No," she promptly replied.

"Well, the hotel is still respectable," said the clerk.

After telling the story, I said, "And that is as far as I want to go with gay stories. Because like the story, my reputation is then still respectable." There is quite a moral here for speakers.

For as we all know those who tell stories must be very careful not to betray public confidence and trust. No one, whose sense of values regarding humor is sound, would attempt to get laughs by spilling over and using stories which suggest the unethical.

The standards of radio and television should be the standards of all public speaking.

IF YOU DON'T LIKE WHAT YOU'RE HEARING

Here's a story a speaker can use if he has any doubts about the audience appreciating what he has to say. It comes from one of the deans of the entertainment world, Eddie Cantor.

On a recent television program Eddie Fisher, the singer, was interviewing the venerable Eddie Cantor about the wealth of his background in show business. It marked his fiftieth year. Cantor agreed it was a long time; he started when he was fifteen and this occasion marked his sixty-fifth birthday. He said down through the years he had met them all including the old timers. He said that at one time he had W. C. Fields as a roommate and added how Fields loved his liquid refreshment.

One time he got drinking so much that the doctor warned him if he didn't quit there was an imminent possibility that it would affect his hearing and he would become deaf.

Eddie continued, "I asked him if he were going to quit and he said that he didn't think so."

"You see it's this way," said Fields, "I like the stuff I've been drinking better than the stuff I've been hearing."

A STORY SHOWS THE IMPORTANCE OF
THE VISUAL SENSE

This story comes from a program of Groucho Marx, the comedian.

A young Sikh had met an attractive American girl who was visiting India. Upon her return to America she wrote him a letter. He was most anxious, of course, to learn what she had to say but he couldn't read English so he secured an interpreter to read the letter for him. Before the interpreter began reading the young Sikh got behind him and covered the reader's ears. Upon being asked why he was covering the ears of the interpreter the Sikh answered, "the letter was written by his attractive American girl friend to him alone, and he didn't want anyone else to hear what she had to say. It was all right for him to read it, but he couldn't listen."

DON'T TAKE THAT DRINK FOR COURAGE

Some speakers, when accepting speaking engagements, worry about giving the speech until the time of the occasion, and then feel the necessity to bolster their morale or to get courage by taking a drink or two, if available, before they speak. It, of course, is not a good practice, and on an ethical basis alone, is not to be condoned in respect to speaking programs. If noticed, as it usually is, it is bad manners, unless alcoholic beverages are served in connection with a banquet program. Even then a speaker will do a better job without any stimulant, in spite of seeming experience to the contrary.

Wasn't it Falstaff, in one of his gayer observations, who remarked that a little wine lubricates the tongue? It may, likewise, make the tongue careless. But it was Homer who summed it up with, ". . . wine can make the sage frolic, and the serious smile . . . And of their wits the wise beguile."

And there have been speakers who, with the aid of a stimulant, have said things which would have been better left unsaid. Here is a story a speaker may tell when he is refusing that proffered drink, or when he is tempted to have one before he speaks.

THIS FELLOW DIDN'T NEED A DRINK

This story was told by Richard Bennett, the well-known stage actor of yesteryear, the father of Constance, Barbara and Joan Bennett, the movie actresses, in a curtain speech after a performance of one of his plays. Curtain speeches were a specialty of the spirited Mr. Bennett. And they were the stock-in-trade of numerous actors of his day.

So may we digress briefly before we come to our story. John Barrymore was prone to take time out from the reading of his lines to cast snide asides at audiences who disturbed him. During the First World War, the eminent British actor Sir Herbert Beerbohm Tree toured this country in Shakespeare's *Henry The Eighth,* and it was one night after he had given a superb performance of the Cardinal Wolsey character in that play that he was moved to give a curtain speech about the Germans and the Kaiser's beastly warfare. He railed on at great length about their submarine warfare and their torpedoeing of all and any ships on the Atlantic, including American ships. His whole purpose was to snap the United States from her lethargy so she would join the Allies. Of course, his was, as he thought, a patriotic motive. We later joined the war, and the Germans torpedoed his ship on his return to England. They didn't get him.

Other actors, for different reasons, have scolded audiences across the footlights in a pretty serious fashion assuming, often in temperament, that this is their sole prerogative and the stage is their personal platform.

LE GALLIENNE STEPS OUT

Some years ago I was introducing Eva Le Gallienne to a Middlebury College audience. She stood in the wings as I was on the stage halfway through the introduction, when the famous actress abruptly ordered me to stop. I returned to the wings and learned she was disturbed because of the many people coming in late. I got started again on the introduction but didn't do too good a job after the interruption.

The great Eva came out, still smarting under the discourtesy of the late comers and spent the first half hour indulging in a scorching, adverse criticism of the audience for its bad manners. And who was to say she was wrong?

But being the fine artist she is, she finally adjusted her feelings and her remarks to a normal mood and gave an inspiring talk on the theater.

And now actor Bennett's story. He told of the widow of a prominent circus press agent who related about the time her husband was with a circus troupe in the West and one of the lions escaped. A posse was formed to track the animal down, but before the search began, the members of the posse stopped at a saloon where they all ordered drinks, all except the press agent. "Come on," he was urged, "enjoy yourself; have a drink with us."

"Not me," he said in a reluctant manner, "Whiskey gives me too much courage."

AND THE SPEAKER SHOULD REFRAIN

And, while not to moralize, the answer of the prospective speaker who on festive occasions is encouraged to drink, should be, "Drinking gives me too much courage."

RICHARD BENNETT MORE THAN A FINE ACTOR

It is not easy to stop our thinking about the actor, Richard Bennett, now that his name has been brought up in connection with these pages. For as Leonard Lyons, the interesting columnist has remarked, "Bennett was more than the foremost actor of his day, he figured in offstage incidents which became legendary."

He was not only a man of talent but of varied and interesting parts, least among them, certainly, was not his high appreciation of the histrionic ability of other actors of his day. As is a common practice of great men, he was able to see the good in others and to praise them.

HE WAS REPLACEABLE

Here is another legend about Bennett. At the Broadway opening some years ago, of one of the many Maxwell Anderson's plays, this time "Key Largo," a gray-haired man walked into the dressing room of the star Paul Muni and said: "You don't know who I am" . . . "Of course I do," replied Muni. "You're Richard Bennett, the greatest actor on the American stage" . . . "I was," replied Bennett, "until tonight."

Here was gracious truth emanating, I'm sure, from the hearts of both men. There are many times in speaking when occasions for expression of the thought contained here, the appreciation of others, can be cited.

Bennett created not only legends but according to writer Lyons, ". . . he also created a show-business dynasty. He was the father of three daughters (previously alluded to) whose fame, beauty, talent and marriages would make the Gabors seem commonplace.

THE PRINCE PLAYS SECOND FIDDLE TO THEATRE FOLK

Constance, Lyons reports, was the first of the daughters to attain stardom. She was wooed in London by a gentleman named Phil Plant and their good friend was the then Prince of Wales. One night they went to the swank "400 Club," a favorite retreat for the prince. The club was overcrowded and the prince said: "Let's go somewhere else. It's too crowded here." . . . "Don't worry," Miss Bennett told the prince. "Phil can get a table anywhere."

THE FEELINGS OF HER NEXT HUSBAND

"After Plant came the Marquis de la Falaise de la Goudraye. Their marriage was shattered by the time the war began. The marquis joined the French army and later escaped from Flanders by wading into the sea to board a rescue ship. He sank beneath the waves, but surfaced each time and struggled on. The extra strength, he said, came from the realization that if he died Constance would get sympathy as the widow of a hero."

Constance Bennett then married Gilbert Roland, the perennial movie actor about whose relations interesting stories have been told. I have not kept up on her present marital status, but in respect to her theatrical activity I know her latest venture is being on tour with a national company of the New York production of "Auntie Mame." More recently I saw her in a *new old* movie on the late television show. It was good to see her.

Joan Bennett, who is married to Walter Wanger, the Hollywood producer, recently starred on Broadway in "Love Me Little." This summer I saw her play opposite Franchot Tone in a most acceptable performance of a television "Playhouse 90," drama.

The third Bennett girl, Barbara, seems to have forsaken the theatre and the movies. She originally married Morton

Downey, had five children, and then, according to the last report, married Addison Randall.

EPILOGUE OF THE BENNETT STORY INCLUDES — ABOVE ALL JOHN BARRYMORE

Additional pages could be devoted to the Bennett story, but it seems well to launch the epilogue here with another story recounted by Leonard Lyons from his *Lyons Den*. No person could be more suitable to serve as its protagonist than that other great actor and character, and Bennett's most important contemporary and, perhaps, zany, the immortal John Barrymore.

"At the Hotel Savoy in London one night Bennett brought John Barrymore to his room, where they both spouted verse until Barrymore suddenly disappeared. Bennett didn't miss him until the next morning. He phoned downstairs and asked to speak to Barrymore. He heard a voice answer: "This is Mr. Barrymore." They had a long talk and then Bennett discovered it hadn't been a phone conversation at all: Barrymore was under his bed."

CHAPTER ELEVEN

About Politicians and Statesmen

There is a moral of all human tales.
— Byron

Among the social and professional groups which constitute or represent a cross section of our society none elicits more concern on the part of people than the field of politics. The political scene represents a sort of national focal point which draws and attracts the interest of all. This common interest is the essence of our democracy—it is our democracy.

The activity of our politicians and statesmen is the most particular phase of this interest. Their activity, at all levels and in all places, seems to be every man's business, but not always his concern. He praises, censors and ridicules them with equal zest, but not always with equal discernment in judgment.

The breadth and universality of interest in political things and personalities, although often superficial, are related to the individual's concern over his economic and social stability. He interprets every political activity as concerned with his welfare; it is vital and, therefore, has high human interest, especially the activity of the political personality.

This is reflected in every media of expression, the newspaper, the radio, television, and every type of periodical from those concerned with general news to the religious.

Political happenings are analyzed and spotlighted from every angle, and the political figure is usually subjected to closest scrutiny and becomes both the sublime and the ridiculous. It has been the common experience of governments, since those which were our ancient prototypes.

Because of this human concern for things and people political, the latter has been the subject and target of writers from the Greek comic dramatist Aristophanes to the modern playwright, Maxwell Anderson. The president, the statesman, the congressman and the cabinet member have been popular subjects and caricatures for our modern stage and movie entertainment, and have been presented with the same high comic sense of the ancient classic writers. Their high human interest value has made them good dramatic fare.

Less popular, but perhaps iconoclastic in intent and purpose, has been the particular use made of our statesmen and political figures in novel and biography. Such writing, while often concerned with the human qualities of their subjects, has had little or no interest in possible humorous touches.

There is one medium, however, which thrives on propagating the humorous and ridiculous to be found in the people of politics, and that is the anecdote or story. Such stories are always available and should be cultivated by every active speaker as potentially useful.

Our statesmen and politicians are not only targets for humorous tales, but many of them are the best storytellers to be found wherever speaking is done. Many of them, of course, pride themselves on the possession of and the ability to tell stories.

The Washington scene itself, which is more than the figurative hub of political activity in America, is the source of much story material about statesmen and politicians. Some of the stories which follow are thus derived. They represent stories about this important group in American life, and stories they have contributed.

Political speakers or speeches, however, are not usually good examples of the speaking style that other speakers should cultivate.

Here is a little tale which pretty well illustrates the idea.

SPEECH BUT NO MEANING

An audience had just listened to several political speakers. Several members had registered particularly on the big and profound words the principal speaker had used, and had agreed that the use of stylish words was more important than what he had to say.

"He's a typical politician," said one. "You know, I think he uses those big words so people won't know what he's talking about. He's afraid that if people knew what he was talking about, they'd know he didn't know what he was talking about."

SMALL WORDS BUT MEANING

Here is a story speakers can use to tell audiences why they use simple words. Tell them as the character in Mark Twain's story did, your tongue can't handle words beyond one syllable.

Mark Twain was discussing the peculiar ways of politics and politicians with a young candidate with political ambitions. Twain was relating the story of Jim Watrous of Missouri, who aspired to serve in the state legislature.

Jim was anxious to make an impression when he spoke and he thought he could do it by indulging in all the big words in the dictionary. As a result his speeches were almost impossible to follow.

Twain relates, "One evening Jim was milking a cow and practicing one of his speeches at the time, when the cow, evidently fed up with his harangue, kicked him in the jaw, causing him to bite off the end of his tongue."

The young political aspirant said, "I suppose that put an end to his political career."

"No," replied Twain. "Because of his shortened tongue he could only use words of one syllable and his speeches were much simpler and so appealed to the farmers and folks generally that he was elected."

I recently heard a public relations officer, who was introduced by name as the speaker of the occasion, respond with a verbose, flowery comment, completely uncalled for, about the fine introduction he was given. It made a very bad impression on the audience and as a result affected the program.

The individual who is not capable of making his remarks plain and unvarnished will never be a good speaker.

He should not do as this politician originally did.

REALLY PREPARED

A young politician, who had "thrown his hat in the ring," was really successful in his first political encounter in being nominated for office. As his friends stood about congratulating him on his nomination to a state office he swelled with pride and showed his happiness.

"Were you surprised to learn you had been nominated?" one of his supporters inquired.

"Was I!" said the not-so-dumb vote-seeker. "I was so surprised that I dropped my acceptance speech."

George Dixon in his column, "On the Scene in Washington," presents this rather interesting story culled from his observations of a former Secretary of War.

Patrick J. Hurley, former Secretary of War and later Ambassador to China, kicked up a terrible diplomatic stink in November, 1945, by suddenly resigning to the accompaniment of charges that the American Embassy staff in China was seeking to arm the Chinese Communists with U. S. lend-lease to destroy the Nationalist government of Chiang Kai-shek.

He returned to this country roaring that American foreign policy was being scuttled from the inside. He was hauled before the Senate Foreign Relations Committee of which Senator Tom Connally of Texas was then chairman. This is General Hurley's own version of what transpired:

Senator Connally tried to bring out that Pat had a habit of fighting with everybody. The solon demanded that he tell about his disagreement with our ex-commander in China, General Joseph W. (Vinegar Joe) Stilwell.

Pat protested he had never had a disagreement with Gen. Stilwell. Connally said: "Never?" And Pat finally admitted: "Well, just once."

The solon pounced on this. "Tell the committee," he ordered, "what it was all about!"

"I don't want to reveal it publicly," demurred Pat. "But if you go into executive session I will tell you." So Connally ordered everyone but committee members out, and as soon as the doors were closed, snapped triumphantly: "Now tell us!"

"Well," roared Pat, "I was having dinner this night in Chungking with General Stilwell and after dinner we listened to a speech coming over shortwave.

"You were the speaker, Senator Connally. The speech was long, tiresome, and windy—such a speech as only you, Senator, can make.

"We suffered in silence for a long while, then General Stilwell turned to me and said: 'That fellow is full of hogwash!'

"I said: 'No, he isn't.' And that, Senator, is the only disagreement we ever had."

I recently heard a speaker tell this story, before he launched into his subject proper. He first observed that public speaking is a precarious business, then announced that he was supposed to have some ideas about the subject on which he was speaking. In fact, he added, he had some definite convictions about the subject which he hoped would cause no misgivings. At any event he hoped there would be no need to go into executive session, but in the event such action was necessary he would be happy if no one accused him of being full of hogwash. But then maybe someone would defend him as Patrick Hurley defended Senator Connally.

A BRITISH STATESMAN ALSO PRESENTS ONE

Sir Arthur Balfour speaking at a dinner in Washington praised the American colored people.

"I often judge American people by this criterion," he said: "If they like colored people, then I know they are likable themselves and vice versa.

"Once I visited Washington a good many years ago. All the hotel waiters were colored then, and I confess I preferred the quaint colored service to the present sophisticated and elaborate service of the whites.

"The day of my arrival, when my waiter, an old colored man with snowy wool, brought me the menu, I put a coin in his hand and said 'Just bring me a good dinner, Uncle.'

"He brought me an exquisite dinner, and during my fortnight's stay we followed out this program daily.

"The day of my departure, as I took leave of him, he said, 'Goodbye, sir, and good luck, and when you or any of your friends what can't read the bill-of-fare comes to Washington, just ask for old Calhoun Clay.' "

A STORY WITH EXTENDED VALUES

The full value of this story exceeds its specific point. And that is its racial implication and particularly the fact that there are some very fine colored people. This thought may have value today in light of the racial prejudice in many quarters. Certainly there are speakers who can express to advantage or reiterate the sentiments of Mr. Balfour.

A STORY SPEAKERS CAN USE

Arthur Larson, assistant to President Eisenhower, and one of the better Washington speakers told this story, when he appeared as speaker at the President's Conference on Occupational Safety in Washington. It poses the question which many speakers ask themselves.

WHY AM I UP HERE?

My position unexpectedly here on the platform reminds me of a story of two Norwegians who had a rather heavy evening of drinking. They were on their way home across the Brooklyn Bridge to Brooklyn. It was a bright moonlit night. The moon was reflected in the water. They were leaning over looking at the river, and one of them, Olie, said, "What is that bright thing down in the water?" And his friend Hansen said, "Well, that is the moon down there. Don't you see the moon?"

"The moon!" said Olie. "Well, if that is the moon down there, what in hell am I doing up here?"

Mr. Larson then added, "This is exactly the way I feel this morning serving in Secretary Mitchell's place, who was unexpectedly and unavoidably required to be out of town and has asked me to extend his greetings to you and make these closing remarks to summarize the conference."

A SENATOR AND A BEAUTY CONTESTANT

In "Capital Scene" George Dixon contributes another. This is the sort of thing that sears a strong man's soul.

Last fall a senator from Idaho was up to his rangetanned ears in work. In addition to legislative duties he had a crushing schedule of administrative work.

Nevertheless, he pushed it all aside to welcome "Miss Idaho" to Washington. He practically turned himself inside out for the young lady.

The beauty contest entrant, privately Miss Phyllis Ralstin of Nez Perce, Idaho, was due to arrive in splendor at National Airport. Senator Welker was there to meet her with a big limousine he had hired with his own money.

The plane was a good hour late. Nevertheless, Senator Welker gave the tardy damsel his best campaign smile when she finally did arrive.

He kept remembering that his desk was piled high with work that shouldn't wait, but he took "Miss Idaho" on a tour of the city. He drove her to Lee House, Blair House, the Lincoln Memorial, the Tomb of the Unknown Soldier (the solon isn't what you'd call the rollicking type) and then up to the Capitol, where he took her to the Senate dining room for lunch.

After lunch he took her on a tour of the capital, let her see the Senate in action and generally gave her the Class-AA treatment usually reserved for visiting potentates.

He almost knocked himself out.

When the beauty contestant was interviewed on a television program that evening and asked how she had spent her day in Washington, she couldn't remember the senator's name.

FOR THE CIVIC-MINDED SPEAKER

This anecdote can move people to laugh because it contains the idea of the beautiful but dumb. Beyond that the average person would dismiss it thinking, "how stupid not to know your senator's name." But in a certain community it was recently revealed that a large number of people did not know their congressman's name.

The story can be effectively used in talks dealing with the voter's responsibility and his indifference regarding political candidates and issues.

CONFUSION OF TERMS

Paul Herzog, a reasonably well-known national and New York state politician, tells an interesting story in connection with his association as chairman of the National Labor Relations Board.

Herzog appeared at a New York state college forum and recounted some of his interesting experiences while he was chairman of the N.L.R.B. The one that particularly impressed him was in connection with a Buffalo strike. The Labor Relations Board office in Washington received the following wire: "Impending strike at Buffalo . . . Urgent, please send medicator at once."

WHEN SPEAKERS FEEL AT HOME

Speakers very often have a desire to tell certain groups or audiences that they feel very much at home in appearing before them. No better way has been found to indicate this than by the use of a well correlated story which may illustrate the idea. Such a sentiment, properly and sincerely expressed, has a fine influence on audience interest. Here are two stories which may serve:

ONE FROM THE MASTER

Churchill's gift for the light touch was an important factor in winning friends and influencing legislators. On one of his previous visits to the United States just before he addressed a joint session of Congress, Franklin D. Roosevelt was worried about the reception. The Prime Minister soon dispelled all doubts about his welcome by giving the impression he felt right at home. He even made isolationists cheer and chuckle by informing Congress: "I cannot help reflecting that if my father had been an American and my mother British instead of the other way around, I might have got here on my own!"

Here is another story told by Arthur Larson, assistant to President Eisenhower, at a celebration held in South Dakota in August 1954:

WHY I FEEL AT HOME

Mr. Larson said, "I feel very much at home at an occasion of this kind. Some of my most vivid recollections are just such open-air celebrations as this. We'd always have them, of course, on the Fourth of July.

"The first such celebration I can remember was when I was five years old. I must explain that like Calvin Coolidge and George M. Cohan, I was born on the Fourth of July. My mother tells me that my arrival ruined her plans for the best picnic she had ever arranged. Well, on my fifth birthday my parents took me to a big outdoor celebration. My head was full of thoughts about the birthday presents I had just received and the achievement of the great milestone—my fifth birthday. I looked around at the flags, the bunting, the band on the bandstand, the fireworks going off, the orator on the platform, and I finally said to my parents . . . , 'This is wonderful, but they really shouldn't have gone to so much trouble.'

"And so, it is no mere formality when I tell you I am glad you asked me to be with you today. I like the Midwest and I like Midwesterners."

A CONGRESSMAN ENJOYS ONE ON THE COLLEGE PRESIDENT

From the title and the point of this story one might think it belongs more logically in a category of stories devoted to lawyers or educators. But insofar as it was told by a statesman, who formerly was a teacher, it has been included in this group.

I heard the story told by Carroll D. Kearns, United States Congressman from Western Pennsylvania, who is on the important House Education Committee, and recently, because of his music ability, has been serving as sort of cultural ambassador. The press has carried stories of his conducting orchestras in faraway places, and the influence, no doubt, has been notable.

Congressman Kearns thinks personalities from the political field, especially Washington, and from the field of entertainment are too often given special attention in the humorous story, while the college president, who is to his mind especially good material, is too often overlooked.

LOWERING THE DIGNITY OF THE COLLEGE PRESIDENT

Three distinguished gentlemen were enjoying each other's company on a trip in the train's club car. They were socializing and became concerned about each other's business and family. One asked of another, "What about your occupation and family?"

"Oh, I'm a college president," came the reply. "I'm married and have one son and he's a lawyer."

"Well, that's most interesting," said the interrogator.

"I'm a college president, too. I'm married. I have one son and he's also a lawyer."

The two men, who had identified themselves as college presidents, turned and looked expectantly at the third man in a complacent attitude which suggested, "Well, try and match that." He seemingly understood the spirit of their expression by the tone of his remarks as he began, "Well, I'm a lawyer. I'm not married," he said, with emphasis, and continued with pointed finality, "I have one son and he's a *college president*."

THE STORY HAS VALUE FOR OTHER PROFESSIONS

Too often the educator, and sometimes the college president, thinks he is society's elite and God's elect, which other professions don't always subscribe to, as in this case, the law and the statesman.

The story then may have possibilities for use by the speaker who is a lawyer, doctor, business executive and others who may wish to have humor at the expense of the sacrosanct college president. Of course, it is an ideal story for other educators who speak and who may wish to cut the college president down to size.

Then again it may be a good story for the college president to use, especially one who doesn't take himself too seriously.

VERMONT'S LIEUTENANT GOVERNOR MIXES POLITICS WITH HUMOR

Robert Stafford, the State of Vermont's Lieutenant Governor, my personal friend and former student, has the reputation of being a good speaker and one whose talks are heightened by the judicious and apt use of the story. During his campaign last year in the interests of his Vermont candidacy, he enhanced his reputation as a political speaker and entertainer by his humor, and at the especial expense of the Democrats. Here is one of his stories, which can be used by political speakers and others as well!

A STORY FOR REPUBLICANS

It is practically a sacrilege to get caught voting the Democratic ticket in Vermont, but Stafford's story concerns one Republican who went astray.

Around the time of the '56 political campaign in Vermont, an old dyed-in-the-wool Republican went up into the mountains to hunt. He got deep in the Green Mountains and was about to stalk his prey when a severe storm broke causing him to take cover. He found shelter in an old hollow tree trunk lying along the ground. He crawled in the trunk, without any difficulty, away from the elements, but noticed the trunk was well rotted. As the storm continued the tree got real water-soaked and started to swell inwardly, crowding the poor hunter into its ever-decreasing hollow. He became frightened lest he would not be able to get out and would die in the log.

Like a person drowning and going down for the third time, the events of his life through the years came to his mind in rapid retrospect.

He thought of the time he cheated at cards, how he had lied to his wife, how he had failed to attend church and other indiscretions of conduct. But his subconscious mind had not unfolded them all. One appeared before him which gave him a staggering blow.

Like a true Vermonter he had always voted the Republican ticket, but now to haunt him came the grim memory of the shameful sin he had committed back in 1932. He had been taken in by the glib talking Franklin D. Roosevelt and the promises of his social legislation program, and he voted the Democratic ticket.

The spectacle of the horrid reminder made him feel so small and so reduced in size that he crawled out of the swollen log without the slightest effort.

CHURCHILL HUMOR AGAIN

Robert Lewis Taylor in his recent biography, *Winston Churchill*, gives an interesting tale revealing the Prime Minister's ready wit.

V.E. Day was Churchill's and England's great day of the war, and Churchill exacted the full spirit of triumph from the crowd as he drove to the House of Commons from 10 Downing Street making his sign of victory. At one point of the journey he realized he had forgotten his cigars and he instructed Inspector Thompson, his bodyguard, to go back and get one. "They expect to see it," he said.

When he finally entered the chamber of legislators, it is reported, "he was given the most tumultous ovation in the history of the assembly."

Several months later, the British voted him out of office, but he seemed to accept the sudden repudiation and at this point he was indifferent to any suggestions of honors.

According to biographer Taylor's story, he declined a dukedom, and upon being offered the Garter remarked:

"Why should I accept the Garter from his Majesty when his people have just given me the boot?"

THE CHURCHILL STORY ALWAYS USEFUL

Anyone who cultivates Churchill's stories for use in speeches is in good company. His stories, while strictly not in the high-laugh category but of the more subtle type, are especially high in human interest appeal. For this reason it should not be difficult to adapt them easily to broad speech uses. The above story is a fine example of the human interest element which makes for ready speech adaptibility.

A LADY STATESMAN USES AMBIGUOUS LANGUAGE

Some time ago, George Dixon, the Washington columnist, relates that he "ran into" the former treasurer of the United States, Georgia Neese Clark, whose name used to be on all our paper money. She said she was living in Richland, Kansas, and he asked her what she was doing there.

"I'm running an elevator," she said.

"I'm indeed sorry about your circumstances," said Dixon, and added, "but into each life some rain must fall."

"Nuts!" snapped back the former treasurer, "it's a very profitable grain elevator."

DON'T BLAME THEM

One of the current magazines contributes this one:

Major Weeks, a spit-and-polish officer with a typical Pentagon assignment, had a high opinion of his own military perfection. He was loudly airing his pet peeve. He claimed that the men in the wartime office he commanded were completely unmilitary.

"They don't work like soldiers," he complained to his young civilian secretary. "They don't look like soldiers or act like soldiers."

The secretary pointed out that the men were mostly recent inductees, trained as infantry replacements rather than desk workers. The major gave an irritated grunt.

"Nonsense!" he snapped. "Just look at them," pointing out the office window to a group leaving the building. "No snap. They don't even walk like military men." And then added in caustic manner, "Who ever told them they were soldiers?"

Turning from the window, the secretary said quietly, "Their draft boards, sir."

ATTORNEY-GENERAL WILLIAM ROGERS

President Eisenhower's appointment in 1957 of William P. Rogers to succeed Herbert Brownell as Attorney General gave happiness to the alumni of Colgate University, for it brought cabinet rank to a graduate of that fine Eastern institution for the first time. Charles Evans Hughes, Secretary of State under two Presidents, spent two years at Colgate but at the beginning of his junior year transferred to Brown because of family reasons.

Rogers is one of the youngest men to serve in a cabinet post. The alumni of Colgate who know him, respect and like Bill Rogers. Of course, in his profession, he has, through the years, established a good record.

In a recent Colgate publication, comment about the new cabinet member runs, "A notably calm, well-balanced and tireless individual, he is also well known for his wit. At a dinner to which he had been invited as the principal speaker, the toastmaster had just introduced Mrs. Rogers when two ladies stood up. After considerable laughter, the new Secretary merely remarked, 'I suppose some of you thought that Ezra Benson (Secretary of Agriculture) was the only Mormon in the Administration.' (One of the ladies was Mrs. Rogers, the other one had misjudged her cue.)"

WHO'S REALLY IMPORTANT?

The Colgate University *Alumni News* reveals another humorous anecdote about its illustrious son. In the December 1957 issue speaking of Rogers it says, ". . . Born in Norfolk, St. Lawrence County, New York, he is the father of three sons and a daughter."

There is a story that one of these boys was taken aside by his father one evening just prior to the time of his appointment when there was considerable telephone traffic between the White House and the Rogers' home. Rogers told his son, "that this was a day he should remember; that it's not often a boy answers the phone when both the President and the Vice-President call the house. 'Yes,' replied the boy, 'but Mickey Mantle hasn't called yet.'"

BOTH ANECDOTES SUITABLE FOR SPEAKERS

It is reasonably obvious that both of these anecdotes about the Attorney General may easily be used or adapted to speech material.

A STORY OF MISTAKEN IDENTITY
ON A NATIONAL BASIS

This story is really concerned with "What Am I?" rather than "Who Am I?" but it has excellent possibilities for use by the speaker. It can serve to point up in a humorous way any reference to the idea of mistaken identity. A speaker may use it at the opening of a talk, if the audience hasn't been well informed about his identity, particularly if the chairman has garbled the introduction in this respect. Of course, here again, there is the need to adapt it properly so it is suitable and not just dragged in.

The story has been told about Dr. You Chan Yang, Korean Ambassador to the United States; in fact, he tells it on himself.

It has been well established since the war in the Korean theater that the Koreans were not only the forgotten race or people; they were also, paradoxically, the-never-known people.

Dr. Yang related he had one day come out of the Korean embassy on one of the less active streets in Washington, and he passed a man who looked at him intently and with a puzzled expression. He thought no more about it until a few days later upon leaving the building the man approached him again, and this time looking at him with equal intent stopped him and said, "I've been wondering about you. You're Chinese, aren't you?"

Dr. Yang answered, "No, I'm not."

"Oh, you're not," said the stranger somewhat disbelievingly. "Now don't tell me." Still studying the Korean, he blurted out, "You're Japanese!"

"No, I'm not," said the Ambassador with some emphasis, "I'm ———."

"No, no, don't tell me," persisted his antagonist, "I know what you are, I know. You're a Filipino."

"No, I'm not a Filipino," said Dr. Yang.

"You're not," in a manner of doubt came the reply.

"No, I'm not," emphasized the statesman.

"Oh, oh, I know, I've got it this time, I know what you are. *You're an Eskimo,*" said the stranger with finality and confidence.

This was too much for Dr. Yang; he just walked off without replying.

This story, if well told, really has appeal. Of course, a Korean telling it may heighten its value, but it still has audience appeal and value for speakers generally.

ABOUT IKE'S GOLF PARTNER—ADMIRAL HALSEY

George Dixon relates that Representative Jack Westland of Washington was playing in a golf foursome which included President Eisenhower and Democratic Senators Stuart Symington, of Missouri, and J. William Fulbright, of Arkansas. According to Dixon, "Along about the 14th hole they got gabbing about World War II. Symington recalled that he had been Secretary of the Air Force and Mr. Eisenhower remembered that he had been connected with the armed forces. Westland said he had been a lieutenant j.g. in the Navy.

"You are playing with a General and an ex-Air Secretary now," said Symington. "I guess you didn't get to play with much top brass when you were a j.g.?"

"Oh, I don't know," shrugged Westland. "I had quite a golfing experience with Admiral 'Bull' Halsey!"

"I played golf with Bull Halsey," interjected Ike.

"I didn't play golf WITH him," said Westland. "I played AT him."

"I was on the carrier INDEPENDENCE," said Westland. "One time we tried to shoot a line across a tanker but the line-throwing gun kept missing. I told my immediate superior: 'Let me tie a line to a golf ball and I'll drop it across that tanker every shot!'

"I got a driving iron. It did the trick—although one of the old chief petty officers darn near choked to death. He kept staring at me and spluttering: 'That's the Navy Reserve for you!' "

President Eisenhower roared. "But what about 'Bull' Halsey?" he persisted.

"The stunt worked so well," said Westland, "that I had a sporting goods company send me a dozen golf balls with a line vulcanized into them. I used them for all the line-throwing from the INDEPENDENCE.

"Everything went well until one day the MISSOURI came alongside and I was ordered to drive a line across it. I wanted to be sure it didn't drop short, so I took a brassie and let go with everything I had.

"Unfortunately the line caught in a splinter on the deck. The ball continued on its flight, wild and free. It landed on the bridge where Admiral Halsey was standing and ricocheted around his startled head."

"What did you do?" panted Senator Symington.

"There is a popular expression in the Navy," replied Representative Westland. "I used it. I said, 'Let's get the hell out of here!' "

A GOOD SPEECH ENDING

Here again is a splendid story a speaker may use to end a speech. There is no question about it possessing definite finality, and easy adaptability to numerous talks.

CHAPTER TWELVE

Miscellaneous Stories—
For Speaking Situations

Though old the thought and oft expressed,
'Tis his at last who says it best.

—Lowell

The selections and stories included in this section have definite value for use in various speech situations which affect either the speaker or his material.

In most cases, the application to speaker or speech is indicated, but it is in no way intended that the stories apply to a single or limited situation. To employ their full use and to realize their potential value assumes some deftness and imagination in public speaking techniques.

There has been limited, but effective and unique use made of some of the material, but there is no doubt about it possessing fresh appeal for speakers. One or two selections included were not born yesterday, but in any use made of them their appeal can be of long and sustained value, for they are, by their nature, in no way trite. If properly employed or expertly woven into speech material all the stories or selections included here should heighten its appeal considerably; for, in the last analysis, effectiveness of material without question rests with the user or speaker.

HAVE SOMETHING TO SAY OR DON'T TRY TO SPEAK

Every person who is called on to speak at a banquet or a similar gathering may not have the desire to say something when he has nothing to say, even though the chairman has been courteous in recognizing him.

Some people want to speak because *they want to say something*, others, the real speakers, speak, because *they have something to say*.

Public speaking is not an exhibition art. So the wise person, even though he has been called on, should not speak if he has no thoughts to communicate to an audience.

Some of the stories or material which follow may be used by the person who feels the urge to say something but hasn't the thoughts. It may help him think up something to say.

THE MORAL, THROUGH HUMOR, TYPE OF STORY

Here are two stories which have unusual value in suggesting the complexity of our modern society, and the intense world situation of which we are a part. The stories on the surface possess considerable humor and yet they have real overtones of value for speakers who wish to impress listeners with serious thoughts about the world today.

There are numerous situations to which good speakers may adapt these stories.

A GREAT HORSE AND LIFE

The story is told by Judge Arthur T. Vanderbilt of the New Jersey Supreme Court. He had been invited to go to Kentucky to speak to the State Bar Association. His hosts had taken him out to visit the famous blue grass farms where the great Kentucky thoroughbred race horses are raised. He was shown a particular spacious pasture where the greatest race horse of modern times, *Man-of-War*, was spending his final days after a great racing career. The judge was taken over to a stable where emblazoned boldly on the front was, "*Man-of-War*." "This is the fastest horse the world has seen," and under it some wag had written "And this is the fastest world a horse has seen."

EMPHASIZING THE SAME IDEA

A fire had broken out somewhere in a hotel. Smoke could be smelled and it wasn't long before the guests saw smoke trailing through the halls and down the staircase.

Upon investigation a room was found on one of the upper floors where smoke was seeping through the door cracks indicating the source of the fire. The door was locked and entrance could not be gained to the room. When the firemen arrived, they chopped down the door. Their hurried entrance was met by a gust of smoke and flames were licking up the curtains in the room.

Looking around the room they realized a person was snugly entrenched under the bed's blankets, thus far totally unaware of the imminent danger or possible tragedy. He was immediately pulled out and dragged into the hall. After a little activity he was brought around, but not completely, as he was sleeping off an earlier drinking affair.

He was shaken by the firemen and they said to him, "Didn't you realize you fell asleep smoking in bed?" In drawling unclear speech, he replied, "I did-n't smoke—in bed." "The room is all ablaze," said the firemen. "What did you do to start the fire?"

"I didn't—start a fire,"- he continued, "It was burning when I came in."

In other words, life was already complex when we got here.

A SENSE OF PROPORTION IN SPEAKING— A GOOD STORY

In some speaking programs where there are several speakers, each must have a proper sense of his own importance. The chairman can't be more important by what he says or by how long he talks than the main speaker, or another speaker can't assume that he is more important than anyone else on the program. Each should respect the other and have a sense of proportion.

A speaker may have this sense and yet feel he is not respecting it. If he feels he may be going over his time limit, or saying more than he is supposed to, he can remove the possible stigma of audience annoyance or ease the situation by the humor of a story. Here is a good story regarding a sense of proportion which dates from World War I:

Not unlike many people of World War II, who realized great profits from certain business enterprises, a certain individual, who is the main character of this story, had done all right for himself in the rabbit-sausage business. He amassed such profits from the new sausage mixture that other sausage manufacturers showed concern for his product. One of his competitors, anxious to learn the secret of the money-making sausage, approached him about the product.

"That rabbit sausage of yours is certainly taking hold with the public," he said. "Tell me, just what are the ingredients? It surely isn't all rabbit meat, is it?" knowing the war scarcity of even rabbit.

"Well, not entirely," came the reply. "You see, I use a little horse meat."

"Horse meat!" exclaimed his questioner, and added, "well, what proportions do you use?"

"Oh, fifty-fifty" came the reply, "one horse, one rabbit."

SPEAKING OF ENGLISHMEN
WHO DON'T UNDERSTAND STORIES

The Dean of Wagner College in Staten Island, New York, feels it isn't only the Englishman who is slow to get the point of a story.

Whenever he is about to tell a story to the college audience he always prefaces it by asking, "Have you heard the story about . . .?" The answer is usually, "No," so he proceeds to tell it.

One time the student body decided to say, "Yes." So the next time the Dean posed his question, "Have you heard the story about . . .?" the students answered "Yes," so the Dean replied, "Good, now you'll understand it."

FOR CHAIRMEN WHO GARBLE NAMES

Aside from the speech chairman who overdoes when he introduces a speaker and engages in the sugary type of comment, there is nothing worse than a speaker being introduced by the wrong name or having the chairman garble his name.

I recently heard a speaker whose name is often mispronounced or is not known, when he is introduced, tell this story:

Before the success of her book, "A Tree Grows in Brooklyn," Betty Smith, the author, had divorced her husband, Joseph Jones. Prior to this they had traveled together extensively. According to Irving Hoffman, the columnist, if the trip was in connection with Betty's work they would use her name when signing the hotel register. If it were just a pleasure trip, they would use her husband's.

On one occasion they couldn't decide the real nature of their trip and, within hearing distance of a startled hotel clerk, the authoress turned to her husband and said, "Which shall it be this time, dear—Smith or Jones?"

WHEN SPEAKERS ARE LATE

I heard a speech program chairman use this story when the speaker he was waiting to introduce walked in just in time to be introduced. A speaker, who is late, may well use

it when he has kept his audience in an uncomfortable position waiting on him.

A CLOSE SHAVE

A Broadway playboy had a closer shave than he bar-
gained for in a local barbershop. His manicure girl was very
beautiful, and he suggested dinner and a show that evening.
"I don't think I ought to," said the girl demurely. "I'm married."

"Ask your husband," suggested the playboy. "I'm sure
he wouldn't mind."

"Ask him yourself," said the girl. "He's shaving you."

A GENTLEMAN IN A CONDITION—WHO DRIVES

Here is a ridiculous story and yet it may have its place
in some talks which point up how ridiculous some people
are who drive cars; those people who think drinking and
driving go together. The story may have been told many
times.

Late one night a man with an unsteady weaving walk
practically fell against his car as he approached it. In his
intoxicated manner he fumbled his keys and tried the impossible task of trying to unlock the car door, but with little
success. He couldn't even find the lock, to say nothing about
whether he had the proper key.

A policeman, who strolled along the sidewalk noticed
the gentleman's antics, approached him and said, "Surely,
my good man, you are not going to try and drive that car,
are you?"

Dazed and without physical stability he looked at the
officer and said in stuttering tones, "N-now, now off-i-cer,
you, you surely don't think I'm in any con-di-tion to walk!"

IN THE SAME CATEGORY

Three buddies walked into a saloon showing the effects of previous celebration. As they approached the bar one of the trio fell down, having reached his limit. He was completely out.

The other two ordered a drink and one of them pointing to the third one on the floor said to the bartender, "He doesn't want anything, he's driving."

A SPEAKER CAN ALWAYS USE THIS ONE

Georgie Jessel, the famous comedian, when he speaks, often replies to a wordy and flowery introduction, especially if it sounds overdone and has the quality of a eulogy, by saying, "For a minute I thought I was dead."

Many speakers feel that introductions are overdone and chairmen often elevate them to undue eminence and importance.

They feel like the boy in this story who, because of his companions' remarks, felt obliged to assume or live up to a high position.

Two members of the English royal family, when they were boys, the Duke of Windsor and the Duke of York wandered off the domains of the royal castle at Buckingham, or wherever it was. They ended up in a village a reasonable distance away. Before long they had taken up with some new companions of the village and became engaged in the rollicking sport of the season, a good snowball fight. In the melee which ensued, several windows in village homes were broken and presently the local police were on the scene, who picked up three boys. With their identity unknown, our royal friends were among them and the three boys were taken to the local police judge.

The judge questioned the boys. "Who are you?" he said to the first boy, who answered, "I'm the Duke of Windsor." "Oh, is that so?" said the doubting officer. "And who are you?" he said to the second boy. "I'm the Duke of York, sir."

"Well, isn't that just fine," the judge replied and turning to the village boy he said, "And just who may you be?"

"Oh, I'll stick with my buddies. I'm the Archbishop of Canterbury."

WORDS OR SPEECH INSPIRATION

Some people who are called on to speak seem to think the only requisite for making an impression is to have words or be fluent, a gift of gab, which is tantamount to saying something, without really having anything to say, or speech inspiration.

This following story seems to convey the idea.

GIVE ME WORDS

A certain speaker said, "When the chairman called on me without warning, I felt I was in the same position as the visiting colored minister from down South who was about to speak before a large congregation of colored folks in Chicago. He asked the church pastor what he should say to the group and was advised to pray to the Lord for inspiration.

"Whereupon he replied: 'No, bruther, it is not inspiration Ah needs, but words to say to your people.' "

SHOULD EVERYONE ATTEMPT TO SPEAK?

Here is one person when called on to speak who felt he was not adequate as a speaker because speaking didn't come naturally. He preferred to leave it to those for whom it is a natural technique. He used a good story to illustrate his point.

DOING WHAT COMES NATURALLY

"I am happy for the confidence placed in me, which allows you to call on me to say a few words.

"The question which always arises in one's mind on such an occasion is, 'what shall I talk about?' The reply one quipster made to the question was, 'talk about a minute.' In more specific language, or in the language of Franklin Delano Roosevelt to his son, 'Be sincere, be brief, be seated.' I can try to follow these three points.

"Actually, I do not consider myself a public speaker, and yet when one hears some people speak with perfect ease and unusual appeal, speaking seems to be a simple matter.

"I don't mean to moralize or instruct, but I am reminded of an incident from the world of sports about which I read, and which I think establishes my point.

"Some years ago Hoot Evers, the Detroit outfielder, was having a bad afternoon playing center field; he had made two or three errors. An enthusiastic fan jumped from his seat in the outfield bleachers, ran out into the field and stood next to Evers. He nudged him, and as the story goes, said, 'move over, I can play this position better than you.' To the fan it looked easy.

That's about it. To the average fan after watching the smooth, easy play of a Joe DiMaggio, playing the outfield, like many other things, it looks easy.

Ethel Barrymore, talking to some young hopefuls of the theater, said: "Yes, acting appears to be easy. You watch an actress on the stage as she goes through her part, so gracefully and with such perfect naturalness that it looks easy. But that grace and naturalness is the result of years of training and practice in technique, and hard work. Yes, good acting appears to be the natural thing, the easy thing, but don't try it unless you are trained to be natural."

"Yes, as the saying goes, 'doing what comes naturally' is what it amounts to. Since I don't think speaking is easy and doesn't come naturally to me, I am going to sit down and listen to the main speaker for whom it is apparently the natural thing."

WHAT ARE YOU WORTH AS A SPEAKER?

Stories and anecdotes are often associated with men prominent in various activities of American life. Such a man is Branch Rickey, a prominent name in baseball for more than twenty-five years and a fine influence in the life of young people, beyond the domain of the game itself. He escaped being included in the book's section on sports.

Up until the last year Rickey's latest active assignment, since the early fifties at least, has been with the Pittsburgh Pirates of the National league in an effort to give Pittsburgh a long awaited pennant. It looks as though Rickey's rebuilding job has just about been completed. As the 1958 season closes the team's standing is the best in years; it is assured of second place and it is still fighting for the pennant spot.

A fine young team, including such boys as Dick Groat, Bill Virdon, Roberto Clemente, Bill Mazeroski, Bob Friend and their spirited field manager, Danny Murtaugh with whom this item is partly concerned.

Danny played second base for the Bucs in 1950 and imbued a losing team with spirit, and even then, presaged his talents for managing. Some years ago Frankie Frisch, the baseball great, said of him:

"He owns the kind of spirit from which ordinary teams become good and good teams become great."

Rickey in 1950 was impressed with Murtaugh, and apparently always has been, including his batting average that year of .294, for he handed him a blank contract for 1951 and, giving him carte blanche, said:

"Put in whatever figure you think you should have," he ordered.

Murtaugh wrote $15,000 and, as he said at the time:

"It was more than I ever got in my life."

Vince Johnson, the Pittsburgh Post-Gazette writer observes, "Danny's salary as Pirate Manager next season (1959) will be a matter of conjecture for sportswriters and of comfort for the Murtaughs."

And you can bet, although the Rickey influence in policy matters for the Pirates may seem passive and behind the scenes, he will have a voice in determining the figure and he'll do all right by his boy, Danny.

And this poses the interesting and important question for speakers, "What are you worth?"

Too many speakers establish their fee in advance, and falsely on the basis of an honorarium rather than their true worth. It might help speaking, in some cases, if speakers were asked to name their price after they had given their speech. They might sense they have been ineffectual or long-winded on some occasions. Too often, true evaluation is lacking. This, of course, applies both ways. Many good speeches are gratuitously given.

TWO SIDES TO THE QUESTION

Do you ever talk to civic groups or community organizations about things to improve your town? Are you inclined to recognize easily the things which annoy and disturb you, such as noisy delivery men? Well, here's an amusing other side to the picture which is not told often enough, but which has its place, even though humorous.

THE MILKMAN COMETH

To paraphrase Eugene O'Neill's play titled, "The Iceman Cometh," there is much to be said about when the milkman cometh. And to use bad English, why does he cometh, so early in the morning with squealing brakes and grinding gears to break our peaceful slumber?

Something should be done about the milkman getting up in the morning with the cows. Before-the-crack-of-dawn deliveries are not necessary to the home in this age.

What is more, the milkman would be spared the indignity of requests made by the housewife, as herein suggested.

THE EARLY BIRD DOES THE TURN

According to the Vancouver Daily Province, a milkman's life is never dull, and the milkmen of this city have learned not to be surprised at any sort of request. The following are actual notes left by customers:

Dear Milkman: When you leave my milk, knock lightly on my bedroom window and wake me. I want you to give me a hand to turn the mattress. P.S. Hope you don't mind.

Dear Milkman: My back door is open. Please put milk in refrigerator, get money out of cup in table drawer and leave change on kitchen table in pennies, because we want to play bingo tonight.

Dear Milkman: When you leave the milk, will you please put coal on the furnace, let the dog out, and put the newspapers inside the screen door? P.S. Don't leave any milk.

ALWAYS POPULAR

"The speaker certainly made a hit tonight," remarked a person who had attended a dinner.

"What did he talk about?" asked an absent one.

"About five minutes," came the reply.

THE BEST AFTER-DINNER SPEECH

"Now I suppose they'll all get up and spout a while," remarked one banquet diner to the man next to him. "Did you ever hear a really good after-dinner speech?"

"Just once. A friend of mine said: 'Waiter, bring me the check.' "

THERE'S HUMOR IN THE SERIOUS

I don't know which group is progressing more to improve and remove the stigma of waiting to be served, the barbers or the doctors, but I'll vote for the barbers. Let's include the doctors in our humorous perspective although our observations may be thin and limited, and we may be damned for including the medics in the same breath with the barbers.

WHY SHOULD THE DOCTORS ESCAPE?

As Moliere the French dramatist says, "Surely the medics have no divine exemption."

In spite of all the good they do, many doctors with their pseudo-professional manner warrant a laugh.

And as Susan Hayworth, the movie actress, says in one of her pictures, in which she portrays Jane Froman, as she pins a flower on the lapel of her doctor's coat, "All doctors should wear a rose to help remove that serious and infallible look they all have."

It seems their worst sin is the way they keep people waiting. In this respect their public relations value is practically negligible. The waiting itself, if it ended there, might be excused; but a group of patients waiting in a doctor's office can, by their complete subservience, create an atmosphere or mood which is literally "out of this world."

It seems almost a sacrilege to enter a doctor's office where a suffcient number of people have established this atmosphere, which they seem to feel the medics must have as befitting their professional dignity.

It has got to be so bad one feels he will be penalized by having an appendix removed, if he is caught saying "hello" to anyone he knows. If he looks at someone, he might be punished by a sudden unaccounted-for attack of high blood pressure.

Because of the surreptitious manner in which people sneak over to the magazine stand to snitch a copy of *Field and Stream, Time,* or a mutilated copy of *Life* or in some cases *The Rotarian* or *The Kiwanis Magazine,* depending on which organization the doctor is a member of, it would be an improvement if they were given their reading matter when the secretary checked them in, to save embarrassment after having taken their seat.

During the war an independent-minded individual entered a crowded elevator, and sensing the strict spirit of conformity to which people were responding he stood in front of the car and in the manner of a command called out, "Everybody will please face to the rear." Everyone responded to the man.

The lack of spirit and the mood which pervades many a doctor's office has more than once put me on the verge of similar behavior. I have felt the urge to announce in somber tones, "We will all stand and I will lead you in singing the "Doxology." Or, perhaps, if this is sacrilegious to sensitive minds, I have thought proposing, "Will you all join hands and we will sing the first verse of 'Blest Be The Tie That Binds.' " To kick the morale completely apart, I have thought of suggesting the singing, by all waiting patients, of "God Bless America."

It's either the religious atmosphere which must be invoked or the patriotic, or the doctors will have to provide a floor show.

And now for a little story which provoked all this:

HE WAITED LONG ENOUGH

I had been sitting in the doctor's waiting room a long time. Every chair was filled and some patients were standing. There was desultory conversation, but after a while a silence fell and we sat waiting—waiting—waiting. Finally an old man stood up wearily and remarked, "Well, guess I'll go home and die a natural death."

SCORE ONE FOR THE MEDICS

When the world's leading medicos were in the United States for the second world cardiology congress much shop talk and many trade jokes were exchanged.

The joke that got the biggest play concerned three surgeons—an American, an Englishman and a Russian. They began arguing as to which had performed the most delicate and complex operation.

The American boasted he'd done a brain job that should go down in surgical history as the most complicated ever attempted. The Englishman pooh-poohed this, saying the honor should be his for an ultra-delicate heart operation.

"And what," they asked the Russian, "was your most difficult operation?"

"I removed a man's tonsils," grunted the Russian.

"But anybody can do that. In our countries it is considered nothing."

"I know, but in my country everybody is afraid to open his mouth so I had to approach it from a different angle."

FAMOUS ARCHITECT DIDN'T INVOKE THE FIFTH AMENDMENT

Frank Lloyd Wright, the famous architect and a well-known individual on the American scene has never, according to columnist E. E. Edgar, in his "Famous Fables" been humble about his talents, which is not an uncommon trait with men of great ability.

Tradition has it that when the committee entrusted with laying the original plans for building New York's great subway set about to get the project started, they approached a famous engineer and asked him to list the names of engineers, in the order of their importance or abilities, to whom the job for the building responsibility might or could be assigned. As the story goes, he prepared and submitted a list with his own name in the number one spot.

The engineer was supposed to have been General George Washington Goethals, but it is apparent he didn't get the assignment although he was engineer for many New York City projects including the development of its harbor.

But back to Frank Lloyd Wright. At one time, when he was testifying in court, he was asked who was the world's greatest architect. Without hesitation, he replied:

"I am."

When he left the courtroom, a friend said to him:

"Couldn't you have been more modest? Did you have to say that?"

"What else could I say?" countered Wright, "I was under oath."

A CONTRADICTION IN GREAT MEN—MODESTY AND SELF-ASSURANCE

This little story about architect Wright, in spite of its humor, brings us nevertheless to an important recognition and yet, a seeming contradiction in the characters of outstanding people, and one worthy of speculation and study for speech purposes. It is, on the one hand, their possession of absolute self-assurance, and, on the other, the revealing of complete humility.

Dr. Harry Emerson Fosdick in his early ministry wrote a small book "The Manhood of The Master" in which he earnestly contemplates this thought in respect to the character of Jesus. But in his commentary he says, the best explanation of this apparent contradiction in fine characters was written by John Ruskin, which Fosdick has interestingly quoted in connection with the idea: "I believe," says Mr. Ruskin, "the first test of a truly great man is his humility. I do not mean by humility doubt of his own power, or hesitation in speaking his opinions, but a right understanding of the relation between what he can do and say, and the rest of the world's doings and sayings. All great men not only know their business but usually know that they know it, and are not only right in their main opinions, but they usually know that they are right in them, only they do not think much of themselves on that account. Arnolfo knows that he can build a good dome at Florence; Albert Durer (the German painter)* writes calmly to one who has found fault with his work, 'It cannot be done better;' Sir Isaac Newton knows that he has worked out a problem or two that would have puzzled anybody else; only they do not expect their fellow men therefore to fall down and worship them. They have a curious undersense of powerlessness, feeling that the power is not in them, but through them, that they could not do or be anything else than God made them, . . ."

On the side of humbleness alone that fine writer, Dr. Fosdick, adds further:

"How instinctively we approve the spirit of a humble man. We think all the more of Mr. Gladstone when he accepts a weighty responsibility, saying: 'The longer I live the more I feel my utter powerlessness in the House of Commons. But my principle is this: never to shrink from any such responsibility when laid upon me by a competent person.' We like Lord Tennyson the better when we learn that he wrote *The Brook*, and then threw it in the wastebasket because he thought it was not good enough to publish. We feel instinctively that the best work will be done by men who are humble, that is, who are teachable and aspiring, who compare themselves with the loftiest ideals and know they have not attained their highest, and who feel that the power by which they do their best work is given to them, not created by them. It is to such that even the world says, 'Come up higher.' "

* The parentheses are the author's.

In this thesis, and with the examples considered and re-vealed above, is some fine thunder for building good speeches.

WHEN YOU DON'T KNOW

As pointed out elsewhere in this book, a good story can usually be put to use by a deft speaker to illustrate a point in his speech, without being dragged in. Here is a story which may apply to a situation where the chairman or speaker doesn't get his facts right or wants to admit to the audience there are some things either of them doesn't know, or under-stand.

This story and the anecdotes which follow are in the dialect and amusing word construction of the "Pennsylvania Dutch," so common to the Eastern counties of that state, and found in such expressions as, "Throw the horse over the fence some hay."

Further interesting evidences are also revealed in the popular song of some time back, "I Warm So Easily, Dance Me Loose, It Shines So Bright The Moon" and a more recent ditty, "Throw Mama From The Train A Kiss, Wave Mama From The Train A Goodbye." One man in particular was responsible for many stories of this type and the spirit asso-ciated with them.

FROM PENNSYLVANIA'S BELOVED POET

Because of his apparently inexhaustible stores of Penn-sylvania Dutch stories, friends used to hang on the late Tom Daly, poet, lecturer and newspaper columnist. He tells the tale of a visit to Emmaus, Pa.

Alighting from the train, Tom spied two natives from

whom he hoped to get direction. "Can you tell me where the spaghetti factory is?" he asked. Both men pondered deeply and then slowly shook their heads. "No," said one of them, "ve dunt know vere dot iss."

So Tom started down the road, followed by the eyes of the two natives. When Tom was about a quarter of a mile away, one of the watchers said to the other, "Maybe he does. Ve'll find out." So they ran after Tom, overtaking him at a turn of the road.

Out of breath, one of them blurted out, "Oxcoose, please. Maybe you mean the macaroni factory, yah?" Tom allowed that maybe he did. "And where," he asked, "is the macaroni factory?" The two natives looked at each other, shook their heads solemnly again, and then the spokesman of the two answered disconsolately. "Ve dunt know vere dot iss also."

A POPULAR DIALECT STORY

Tom Daly tells, too, about the still prevalent custom around Allentown, Pa., of the butcher selling meat from a wagon and attracting his customer's attention by blowing a horn. One hausfrau, after a lot of trouble, had succeeded in putting the baby to sleep. Just as she tucked the baby in the crib she heard the wheel creakings that were a preliminary to the butcher's toot. She rushed to the stoop just as the butcher had the horn to his lips. "Don't horn!" she called. "You'll blow the baby awake!"

SOME INTERESTING PENNSYLVANIA PROVINCIALISMS

And speaking of Pennsylvania Dutch stories or sayings, which, for the most part, come out of the three eastern counties, Lancaster, Berks and Lehigh, many have been circu-

lating by word of mouth for as long as two centuries. Usually
the meaning of these expressions is clear in spite of an occasional resemblance to paradox.

In this language "all" means all gone, exhausted or
disappeared. "The bread is all," someone observed, expresses
in four words the thought contained in the speech that made
Ethel Barrymore famous—"That's all there is; there isn't
any more." You will, perhaps, remember the Broadway play,
"Papa is All," built around the same idea. An expression
which sounds amusing and implies the same meaning of
"all," I have heard on several occasions:

"When the little red house goes by, the train is all,"
meaning that the caboose is the end of the train.

Commonly used in Pennsylvania is "He wants in; the
dog wants out," meaning, "He wants to come in; the dog
wants to go out."

A girl was invited to a party. In perplexity her mother
confided to a neighbor. "I don't know what I'll wear on her."
The neighbor in the Pennsylvania Dutch country knew exactly
what was meant, as would others.

One of the most appealing little anecdotes belonging to
this group concerns the girl who was told to call her brother
for supper. Several students I have known from the Pittsburgh area refuse to see anything unusual about it as they
claim it is used in their homes. Here it is:

"Johnny, supper's ready. Ma's on the table, Pa's half et,
come in and eat yourself."

Vacation is an "off" period, a time "off" from work. So

when a workman or a schoolteacher says, "My off is on," you know that vacation has started for the speaker.

SIGNS OF OPTIMISM?

Some signs are ambiguous and misleading. They may be construed or interpreted as encouraging and suggest optimism about what is to come, or, conversely, they may suggest not to be too optimistic about the future.

Here is a story which can be most effectively used to point out that indications cannot always be construed to be hopeful ones or vice versa.

It was told by a college president who claimed it had respectable lineage because it had been told at a conference of theologians.

The two young sons of a young couple were the subject of much concern because of their diverse natures and behavior.

One little chap was a happy, contented, little fellow always agreeable and happy about what his parents did for him. The other little fellow, on the other hand, was always disagreeable, mean and disgruntled about whatever was done for him. Their ways had developed into such a pattern the parents realized they needed help, so they decided to visit a psychiatrist.

After listening to their story about the boys, the psychiatrist made what seemed to be a radical proposal for dealing with the problem.

He said in spite of the different attitudes manifested by the boys there was only one way to handle it. Give the disgruntled little boy everything he wanted, and as Christmas was approaching just shower him with gifts.

Give the happy little chap nothing at all. And for Christmas make the contrast noticeable by practically showing disregard and meanness toward him. Give him something which had no semblance of a gift. He suggested they go to a stable and get him a small bucket of horse manure which would serve.

Christmas morning arrived and there was the mean, disagreeable child surrounded by gifts. He had a new bicycle, a set of trains, an air rifle and other things.

He was greeted and asked if he were having a nice Christmas and enjoying his gifts. In his usual complaining manner, he whined that he didn't like the bicycle he got, and he got the wrong trains.

Just then the other little fellow entered the room, carrying his little pail of manure. He was smiling and seemed happy, so he was wished a Merry Christmas and asked what he got for Christmas.

"Well," he said pointing to his little pail of manure, "I think I got a pony, but I haven't found it yet."

DR. FOSDICK'S STORY HAS SPEECH VALUE

Included in his fine autobiography, "The Living of These Days," Harry Fosdick relates a little anecdote which has meaning for all of us.

Speaking of the years during his early ministry at Montclair, N. J., he comments on the play and fun which eased his days and kept his spirits buoyant. He says, "music and the theater helped a lot—and golf helped too."

One Saturday he picked up a game of golf with a stranger and they finished with a tie, so the stranger, not knowing Fosdick was a clergyman, suggested another game the next morning, which was Sunday, to settle the matter. Fosdick told him he could never play on a Sunday because he had a job which compelled him to work that day. "What kind of a job is that?" the golfer asked. "What the hell do you do on Sunday mornings?" Fosdick replied, that was a good question, which he had often asked himself. He suggested the stranger come to the First Baptist Church some Sunday morning to discover the answer.

Of course, this is a good question for anyone, "What the hell do you do on Sunday mornings?" Or at any time for that matter. The story is ideally suited for speeches.

Goodreds, Vincent Spencer, 1896-

    Good stories and how to tell them; a collection of appropriate stories for speakers with instructions about the best way to tell them. Minneapolis, T. S. Denison [1958, c1954]

249 p.   24 cm.

1. Story-telling. 2. Anecdotes.   I. Title.

PN4193.I 5G6   808.5   58—11750 ‡

Library of Congress

Goshen Public Library

Any resident of the city, or student in its public schools or college may draw books from this library.

New fiction is marked Seven Days and is not renewable.

Other books may be kept Fourteen Days and renewed once unless otherwise indicated.

A fine of two cents a day will be charged for each Fourteen Day book, and Five cents a day for each Seven Day book kept overtime, Sundays and holidays included.

Books lost or damaged must be paid for by the patron.